Back to the Red Road

BACK TO THE RED ROAD

A Story of Survival, Redemption and Love

FLORENCE KAEFER

AND EDWARD GAMBLIN

CAITLIN PRESS

Caitlin Press Inc.
8100 Alderwood Road,
Halfmoon Bay, BC V0N 1Y1
www.caitlin-press.com

Edit by Barbara Pulling, copy-edit by Kathleen Fraser.
Edward Gamblin's song lyrics reprinted with the permission of Red Road Music.
Text and cover design by Vici Johnstone.
Map of Manitoba by Natural Resources Canada (The Atlas of Canada) [CC-BY-SA-3.0
(http://creativecommons.org/licenses/by-sa/3.0)], via Wikimedia Commons
Printed in Canada

Caitlin Press Inc. acknowledges financial support from the Government of
Canada through the Canada Book Fund and the Canada Council for the Arts,
and from the Province of British Columbia through the British Columbia Arts
Council and the Book Publisher's Tax Credit.

Canada Council   Conseil des Arts
for the Arts   du Canada

BRITISH COLUMBIA
ARTS COUNCIL

Library and Archives Canada Cataloguing in Publication
Kaefer, Florence, 1935-, author
    Back to the red road : a story of survival, redemption
and love / Florence Kaefer, Edward Gamblin.
ISBN 978-1-927575-37-6 (pbk.)
    1. Kaefer, Florence, 1935-. 2. Gamblin, Edward. 3. Norway
House Indian Residential School (Norway House, Man.)—History.
4. Indians of North America—Manitoba--Residential schools.
5. Abused Indian children—Manitoba. 6. Cree Indians—Education—
Manitoba. 7. Teachers—Manitoba—Biography. 8. Native musicians—
Canada—Biography. 9. Cree Indians—Biography.
I. Gamblin, Edward, author II. Title.
    E96.65.M35K33 2014   371.829'97323071271   C2014-900484-2

This book is dedicated to all residential school survivors and their families.

Contents

Dear Edward,

May the Creator, the Grandmothers and Grandfathers watch over your grave. May they send soft winter snowflakes and place sparkling hoarfrost on the trees around your sacred space beside your beloved Aurelia.

May wildflowers grow beside the fence and among the graves. The wolf and her cubs will silently walk near and stop to listen for spiritual voices and distant drums. She will lie by your grave and remember she is your guardian. A ladybug will alight upon your cross.

May eagles swoop down to earth and lift you up to soar on the air currents, so that you can view all of your Creator's world.

—Florence

Preface

When immigrants came to this land, which they later named Canada, the First People had already been here for thousands of years. Their cultures provided a pristine environment of pure water, fresh air, abundant food and every necessity for life. They welcomed the immigrants along the St. Lawrence River the first winter, saving their lives with a cure for scurvy. In the spring the immigrant Cartier kidnapped the chief's sons and took them to France, where they later died.

Immigrants kept coming by the thousands, disregarding the Original People, destroying their resources and forcing them away from the richest parts of the land. Finally, the immigrants took away the most precious resources of the First People: their children.

In 1954, when I was nineteen, I accepted a job as a teacher at the United Church Residential School in Norway House, Manitoba. Unaware of the difficult conditions the students were enduring, my fellow teachers and I tried to nurture a school full of lonely and homesick young children.

After a few years, I married and moved away to Vancouver Island where I continued to teach, but often thought of the children at Norway House. Many years later, in 2004, I reconnected with one of my students, Edward Gamblin, who had been a bright and seemingly happy young child. I was horrified and deeply saddened when he told me of the abuse he had suffered at the residential school and how the government had erased his cultural identity. Edward and I grew very close over the years. We developed a special bond and eventually he became my tradition-ally adopted son and I his mother.

Edward's life was a tributary that joined mine at a special time in Canadian history—the time of the apology to Indian resi-dential school students. As Victoria Freeman writes in her book *Distant Relations: How My Ancestors Colonized North America,* "I can't speak for Americans, but I know that we Canadians like to consider ourselves benevolent defenders of human rights. It is hard to admit that our modern, liberal democracy has been built upon the destruction of aboriginal nations and cultural identity..."[1]

Edward spoke out publicly about the abuse and racism his people experienced and that still exists in Canada today. He wrote songs, gave interviews, conducted healing circles and began to write a book. Like trickles of water melting from a glacier, Edward and many First Nations people have found their voice and their stories are beginning to flow like a raging river.

When Edward died in 2010, I wondered how I could live without him. In the short years we had together his warmth and gentle nature had such an effect on me. To help me through the tragedy of his death, I decided to write my own story to help him complete the book that he began but never had a chance to finish. I had never written a book before, but for as long as people read it, Edward will live on, so I knew I had to try.

Edward Gamblin left us his stories, his love and his music. His songs remain meaningful and touching, expressing his deepest personal feelings and the feelings of the people he met throughout his life. His melodic, rhythmic and steady beat made it impossible for his audience to sit still and his words often moved them to tears. Regrettably, I never had the pleasure of attending one of Edward's live performances, but his music is in my heart as I dance around the kitchen to his wonderful songs.

Without Edward here to help me I have done my best to remember and write our story. His picture sits on the table beside me as I reread letters, emails and cards and remember our conversations and special talks in the hospital room in Winnipeg. Edward once signed a letter to me, "May the light shine on every path you walk." That light will guide me now.

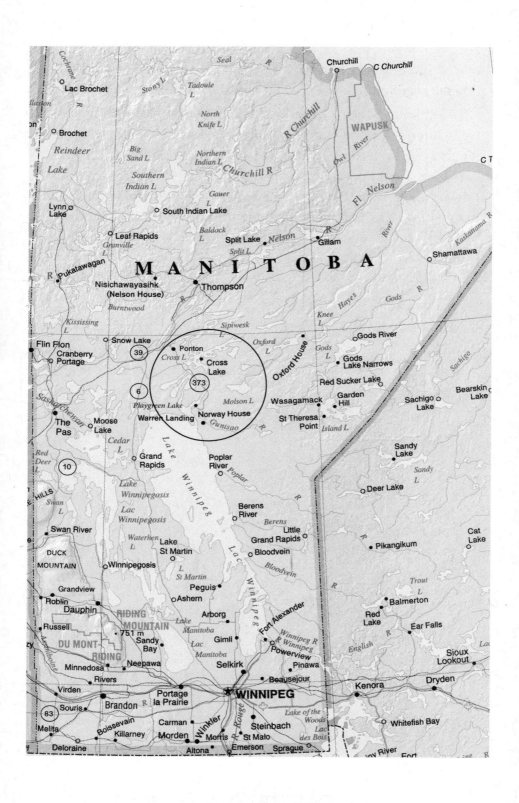

Chapter 1

Florence's Story: The Last Breath

It's July 27, 2010. I phone the Health Sciences Centre in Winnipeg and ask for the desk on GD4.

"Could I speak to Edward Gamblin's nurse?"

"Gamblin's nurse? Speaking."

"How is Edward today?"

"The prognosis is very poor. He is aspirating—fluid is going into his lungs."

"Do you think he is dying?"

"Yes, quite possibly. He is on life support systems; comfort care only."

"Could you please let me know if his condition changes? My name is Florence Kaefer, and I'm Edward's traditionally adoptive mother."

"Are you on good terms with the daughters?"

"Yes."

"Then I will ask one of the family to call you. They are all here."

My heart pounding, I hang up. I cry and cry. Then I phone my friend Stephie in Nova Scotia and sob some more. Stephie Tarnowsky worked with me at Norway House and she knows how much Edward means to me, so we talk and talk. She helps me calm down.

I'm all alone, not knowing what to do. Then an angel phones. It's my friend Jessie, who says, "You sound tired. Are you okay?"

"I'm not okay. Edward is dying."

Jessie comes right over to comfort me, but as soon as she leaves I begin crying again, my head down on the table. When the phone rings, I rush to answer, hands shaking.

"This is Jared," Edward's son says tearfully. "My dad passed away a few minutes ago."

Through my sobs, I say, "We'll all have to be brave." It's the only thing I can think of, but I realize one does not need to be brave in such a situation. Poor Jared. He's only sixteen.

Jared's older sister, Angelique, gets on the phone. "We want you to come to Norway House. Dad's wake will be this Wednesday and Thursday, and his funeral on Friday or Saturday."

"Yes, I'll come."

After I finish talking to Angelique, I phone my daughter-in-law, Tansy, my son Glenn's partner. She and my younger son, Ian, will stop by my place after work. Next I contact my sister Lorna in Morden, Manitoba, and she asks if I'd like her to come along to Norway House.

"Yes, that would be wonderful. This is going to be so sad and difficult."

Tansy, my competent, always available travel agent, arranges my flight from Comox, British Columbia, to Winnipeg. Lorna and I will meet there at the Perimeter Air terminal; her husband will drive her down. We'll fly up to Norway House together, arriving Thursday afternoon.

After the arrangements have been made, and Tansy and Ian have gone home, I contact Harold Harry, a long-time friend who is First Nations and lives here in Courtenay. He'd met Edward and Edward's wife, Aurelia, when they visited me. Harold tells me he'll perform a pipe ceremony at the same time as Edward's funeral and asks me to inform him of the day and time. The pipe he will use is from Pipestone, Minnesota, where for a thousand years people have quarried catlinite, a reddish stone used for pipe making by the Ojibway, Lakota, Cheyenne and Blackfoot peoples. The place is holy ground where warring nations laid down their arms and smoked the pipe together, united in reverence for the Great Spirit. A Lakota story says the first pipe was brought by White Buffalo Woman, a messenger from the Great Spirit, thus forming a link between those on Earth and the Spirit World. She showed people how to pray with the pipe, which is called a Chanupa. Edward also had a pipe he'd made from this special stone collected in Pipestone.

I don't want to go to Norway House for your funeral, Edward. I don't want this. I want to go back and sit with you on your deck, talking as we watch the eagles soar in a big circle above your house, like we did just a short time ago. I can't believe you are dead.

As I struggle to write a sympathy card for Edward's family, the phone rings. It's Mary Starodub, her warm, caring voice expresses her condolences. Mary is an old friend of Stephie's, and we've become friends since she graciously offered to let me stay at her house when I'm travelling to and from Norway House.

I feel so sad as I look at the picture of Edward and Aurelia taped to my teak kitchen cabinet, where I display so many other pictures of my former students. I took the picture when they visited me two years back. Edward looks so healthy and handsome with his grey hair, moustache, glasses darkened by the sun and quintessential cap. He wears the small silver inukshuk he purchased at the Royal BC Museum proudly on his jacket. And now both of them are gone.

Packing for a trip is never one of my favourite activities. I pack my silver and black jacket for the funeral and the feather trimmed with leather and red cloth that Edward gave me years ago to hold when I am nervous.

Now I'm ready to walk another painful stretch of the Good Red Road, the Road of the Sacred Wheel. As Ojibway author Richard Wagamese writes in his novel *Dream Wheels,* "The old ones say that the path of a true human being is a Red Road. It's a blood colour. Like blood it flows out of our histories bearing within it the codes and secrets of our histories, invisible urgings and desires spawned in generations past. Because of that it is a difficult path and only the most courageous and purest of heart have the humility to walk it."[1]

Tansy picks me up at 4:30 the next morning and sees me safely onto my flight out of Comox. Out over the Georgia Strait, across the snow-capped, rugged Rocky Mountains, over the endless green prairies and finally down into my hometown of Winnipeg, along the banks of the Red and Assiniboine rivers. Lorna and her daughter-in-law, Patty, are waiting at Perimeter Air to meet me, and there Lorna and I walk out onto the tarmac to board a small green and white plane destined for Norway House. At the foot of the steps we are given soft foam plugs that we nudge into our ears against the noise. The engine roars as we taxi a long way out on the runway. I wonder how my big sister Lorna will enjoy her first flight in a bush plane. As we take off, the engine roars even louder and soon we are off the ground, swinging a bit from side to side, then steady on north, flying above the immense, steel-blue Lake Winnipeg.

Before long I have a lump in my throat. I know I'll soon see the familiar Nelson River beginning its journey to Hudson Bay, the Gunisao River, a tributary, and then Playgreen Lake. The roads and houses stretch alongside the river joining the larger lake to Little Playgreen Lake. And as we fly lower I pick out the old Hudson's Bay fort, and then cars and trucks. Our sturdy plane turns down, down and then there's the bump as we land. As we disembark and walk into the small terminal, I remember an earlier trip, not so long ago, when Jared met me outside the door to take my bag. Inside was Edward in his black leather jacket and cap, sitting in his wheelchair. I bent to hug him, and we greeted one another in our usual way.

"Mom, so good to see you."

"Son."

But it is not Edward who greets me, but his sisters, Joyce and Cindy. They give us hugs mixed with tears and help us with our bags. We are off down the familiar road to the York Boat Inn in Rossville, the northern part of the Norway House reserve.

Joyce drops us off to check in. After we've done that, Lorna and I walk across a bleak, treeless area to Rossville's only restaurant. Once I asked Edward why there were no trees anymore. The Norway House of 1954 had trees, I remembered. He explained that some young people had been sniffing gas in among the trees, so the Council had the trees removed. Edward said that had cut down on the problem considerably, but I wish the situation with the youth could have been solved differently. This area must be cold and miserable during winter storms.

Soon after lunch, Joyce phones and says she'll pick us up. As we drive along the long, straight road toward Edward's place, Joyce tells us her brother's remains will be flown to Norway House tomorrow with Edward's oldest daughter, Candida, and his son Jared accompanying him.

As I enter Edward's familiar, love-filled home, I remember the first time I came to visit. The room brimmed with sunshine, and in one window was a large aquarium filled with shimmering water and varied goldfish. Today is a grey day, though, and people are working around the big oak dining table, which is adorned with a winsome centrepiece of blue and yellow paper flowers. I slip around to the end of the table, where Edward's daughters Jane and Angelique are busy. We hug and cry together. I see Lorna watching me; for the first time, I think, she's realized just how completely Edward's family has become mine. Others are there around the table. April, Joyce's daughter-in-law, a confident, pleasant young woman, is busy putting pictures into silver frames for the Remembrance Table at the church. There are some of Edward alone, some with Aurelia, some of the whole family. And there is one early photo of Edward with his band. The four of them look like intense, energetic rock 'n' rollers. Edward is obviously the leader, though he's also the shortest.

"This one is for you," April says, handing me a portrait of Edward wearing his cap and dark glasses.

Jane turns to me. "Will you do my dad's eulogy? I just can't."

I am lost for words, and I look to Lorna for support. My heart skips a beat, but I say, "Yes, it will be an honour."

Admiring the centrepiece on the table, I ask, "April, could I have a wreath made to honour Edward?"

"I'll phone and inquire."

"I'd like it to be red and white, since Edward, as my adopted son, is also part of the Kaefer family, and our name in German means 'ladybug.'"

"Yes, I'm sure that will be fine."

Jane has turned her attention to writing Edward's obituary for the *Winnipeg Free Press*.

Before Angelique drives Lorna and me back to the York Boat Inn, I have a visit with my all-time favourite dog, Edward's Fifty. I have such a soft spot for him. Fifty is a golden brown, shaggy-haired, happy dog with adoring amber eyes. He always welcomes an ear rub and a conversation, tongue hanging out, tail wagging.

Back at the Inn, as I settle in for the night, thoughts, memories and visions flow through my mind. I imagine giving the eulogy in the beautiful new ecumenical church, built out on the point, beside the old James Evans Memorial Church where Edward and Aurelia were married. The shock of Edward's unexpected death haunts me—I somehow believed he'd recover. Eventually I fall asleep.

Chapter 2

Florence's Story: Distant Drumming

It was June 1954, and my one-year teacher training program at the Provincial Normal School in Tuxedo, Manitoba, was rapidly coming to a close. Everyone in my class, which we'd dubbed "J for Jabberwocky," was talking about where they planned to teach in September. I was undecided.

Every morning we had assembly, presided over by our tall, beloved principal, Mr. Chidley. Amazingly, he knew all 477 of us by name. This particular morning, he was joined on stage by Reverend Kenneth McLeod, who was looking for elementary teachers for a new United Church Indian Residential School in Norway House. I was intrigued. My mother had always shown a keen interest in ending discrimination. She'd read *Uncle Tom's Cabin* and works by the "Mohawk Princess," Pauline Johnson, such as her novel *The Shagganappi.* I'd grown up loving Johnson's poem, "The Song My Paddle Sings," best of all.

And up on the hills against the sky
A fir tree rocking its lullaby
Swings, swings,
Its emerald wings,
Swelling the song my paddle sings.[1]

When the assembly was over, I went directly to Reverend McLeod and indicated my interest in going to Norway House. He hired me on the spot to teach grade 3. He recruited Stephie that day too. He told both of us that Mrs. McLeod would like to take us out for lunch.

Stephie and I were in different classes, and we didn't particularly like each other. As we'd discover when we later compared notes, she thought I was a stuck-up snob, and I thought she was a loud-mouthed show-off. However, we both met Mrs. McLeod for lunch at T. Eaton Co.'s elegant white-tablecloth, silver-service dining room. When Mrs. McLeod said pleasantly, "Of course you two will want to room together," we both managed to politely reply, "Yes, we would." We betrayed no sign that each of us was grumbling to herself, "How did I get myself into this?"

I thought my kind, selfless mother would be proud of the choice I'd made, though I was the youngest in our family and I knew she'd miss me. She'd be alone now, since my two sisters were already in training to be nurses. On her own, my mother had managed to give the three of us an education and careers we could fall back on if our marriages failed, as hers had. She supported us and then let us go to fulfill our dreams.

Mother helped me over the summer to prepare to leave home for the first time and go north to teach. She had Mrs. Grey, a local seamstress, make me a special Ancient Sutherland tartan wool suit with a fitted mid-length jacket and a pleated skirt. The tartan had a warm blue background interwoven with greens, reds and yellows. I loved it.

Before I left, I paid a visit to my aunt Hannah and my uncle, the Reverend Henry Sweet. They had served First Nations people on the Red Pheasant Reserve in Saskatchewan, and when I told my aunt I was going to teach First Nations children, her only advice was, "Be kind to them." Aunt Hannah's younger sister was Nellie McClung, the famous writer, politician and suffragette, and she herself was a respected high school teacher who often gave lectures on literature that were broadcast on CBC radio. I never forgot that advice.

As a very young child, I'd lived with my family in a small log cabin my parents had built in Spirit River, Alberta. People from the Dane-zaa Nation lived close by. Mother bought moccasins from them and invited them into our home if they were travelling on cold, snowy nights to or from their homes hidden in the woods. One time it was a group of women who were travelling to Grande Prairie to witness their men on trial there. Once I'd heard distant drumming and strange voices in the distance. Little did I know that, many years later, that drumming would become an important part of my life.

By late August my small brown trunk was tightly packed with all I supposed I'd need at my first teaching position: favourite children's books, among them the Uncle Remus stories; Pauline Johnson's *Flint and Feather;* a book called *Totem, Tipi and Tumpline: Stories of Canadian Indians;* and warm things, like mitts, a toque and red long johns. Although Norway House is actually in the middle of Manitoba, I believed I was going to the Far North.

The day to leave arrived. My mother, my sister Lorna and my brother-in-law Gerald drove me first to Selkirk, fifty kilometres north of Winnipeg. From there I was scheduled to take the boat down the Red River into Lake Winnipeg and then north to Norway House. We gathered on a dock in Selkirk. The SS *Keenora* was an elegant white four-deck steamship, with lifeboats on the third deck; below them were rows of windows that curved around the bow. I saw that Stephie was here with her family, too, but we indicated only polite recognition of one another. Around us, workers, many of them First Nations, were busy loading barrels of gasoline,

Stephie Tarnowski and Florence leaving Selkirk on the SS *Keenora* in August 1954. They are off to their first teaching job at the United Church Norway House Indian Residential School.

25

flats of groceries, boxes tied with rope, trunks, suitcases and oxygen tanks onto the boat, carrying them up a wide gangplank or hoisting them into an opening at the bow. These goods, I would learn, were destined to be delivered to isolated communities along the shores of Lake Winnipeg, Berens River and Grand Rapids.

The boat was scheduled to leave at 6:00 p.m., but we needn't have rushed to get there. It was hours later before, finally, the big gangplank was hauled in, the front openings closed and a small gangplank set up at the passengers' entrance. It was time to go. I said an emotional goodbye to my family, especially my mother, and up the steps I went, turning for one last wave at the top.

This was the first ship I'd ever been on. Old sardine cans converted into ashtrays were conveniently placed on ledges all along the red Persian-carpeted hallway. Down the hall was an elegant dining room with dark mahogany tables and chairs, a sideboard and a piano. The white tablecloths on the sideboard and the doilies on the piano made the room look grand. There were fine views from the big windows facing out onto the river and countryside. Already, I could hardly wait for breakfast.

What a pleasant evening it was as the ship gently moved out into the Red River, travelling north. Stephie and I had found one another on board, and we headed eagerly out on deck, pulling up two deck chairs. Could this be the first sign of friendship as we set off into the unknown together? Soft prairie breezes, the freshest of air, mixed with the exhaust coming from the ship's engine. The sturdy SS *Keenora* wound its way through Netley-Libau Marsh, famous for duck and goose hunting. Numberless muddy branches of this huge wetland spread out into the spectacular delta where the Red River emptied into Lake Winnipeg. The word "Winnipeg" meant "muddy waters" in Cree, I knew, and the lake itself was quite shallow in places. It was also 416 kilometres in length, so we were in for a long journey, two nights on board.

The "o-kay-lay" notes of red-winged blackbirds showing off their flashing red epaulettes as they tottered on the slender reeds, the startled sounds made by multicoloured ducks as they took off, and the cries of seagulls in the distance delighted us. The golden hue of the diminishing sun gave the scene an exuberant, spiritual cast. I had been a member of the Young United Church Choir for four years, and the words of a familiar hymn came to mind: "This is my Father's world, and to my listening ears all nature sings, and round me rings the music of the spheres." It was definitely a new world for a young city woman like me.

As the determined *Keenora* chugged its way out of the delta into vast Lake Winnipeg, the waves stroking the boat grew stronger, gently rocking us up and down. The breeze changed to a clement wind. The setting sun was illuminating the sky with mauves and greens when I saw the first star and made a silent wish. "I wish I may, I wish I might be a very good teacher."

It began to get chilly, so Stephie and I made our way down worn steps, holding onto the railing as the ship rocked some more. We swayed down the narrow passageway to a cabin marked No. 5. Ours! Inside, the space was very small: bunk beds covered in homemade patchwork quilts, hangers on a single rod, a small dresser and a pull-on light beside each bunk. Hardly a luxury liner! But once we were curled up in bed we enjoyed the ship's graceful forward momentum. As we lay in the darkness, Stephie and I talked a little. Maybe I would grow to like her, I thought. I wondered what teaching would be like. Would I be able to do this big job? I thought of Mom's favourite saying: "Just do your best, and no one can ask anything more of you." Yes, I would certainly try my best.

Chapter 3 🪶

Florence's Story: Our New School

Stephie and I awoke on the second morning to a weird sensation: the ship had stopped. From the hallway came sounds of people talking excitedly and objects being bumped around. A loud knock on our door was followed by a *Keenora* crew member shouting: "You two—get up! Everyone is disembarking to board a smaller boat that goes downriver to Norway House."

Stephie and I flew into our clothes, threw our nighties into our suitcases and stumbled out the door, down the hall and up the stairs. We were among the last passengers to leave the *Keenora* and board the new vessel.

Once we'd stopped giggling and calmed down, we could see that the *Chickama II* was a fine boat, with flags front and back and a canopy that covered comfortable seats, railings and two life-boats. From the bow, we had a spectacular view of a narrow dark river with rocks and swamp spruce on either side, exuding a mysterious feeling of solitude. This was the Jack River, the birthplace of that mighty northern river, the Nelson.

In the open spaces along the river, insects and birds hovered over grasses, small shrubs and brown muskeg. A few modest log cabins stood back from the water, connected by paths to small docks. One appeared to be some kind of store, with people coming and going. A thin church steeple emerged first from the dark spruce forest, and finally an elaborately decorated Catholic Church came into full view. We passed through a narrow stretch of river that gave us a good view of the gate and jailhouse of the historic Hudson's Bay Company fort. Finally, the *Chickama II* sailed out into island-dotted Little Playgreen Lake. Off in the distance, we could see a small church on a point. Once we'd rounded that point, we were there. The *Chickama II* landed at a large dock crowded with First Nations people in dark clothes. A man with bright red hair stood out. He turned out to be the Hudson's Bay clerk, Jack Witty. We had arrived in the community of Rossville, part of the Norway House reserve, and the place where our new school was located.

The United Church minister, Reverend Ibb Avery, had come to meet Stephie and me, and he invited us up to the manse right away. There were no cars or buses; here, it seemed, everyone walked to wherever they were going. The manse, a small house

The SS *Keenora* and *Chickama II* at Warren's Landing near Norway House.

Norway House Indian Residential School burnt down twice, first in 1913 and again in 1946. The school was rebuilt both times. This new building (above) was opened in 1954.

out on the point near the church, was very simply furnished, and we were greeted there by beautiful Min Avery, Ibb's wife, who offered us a welcome cup of tea. I was shocked to see that in the wedding picture on the mantelpiece, Ibb was with a different bride—it turned out Ibb had a twin brother. Ibb was a great joker, we'd learn, and a very persuasive fellow. When I foolishly told him I sang in the Young United Church Choir in Winnipeg, he responded, "You will sing a solo for us on Sunday." When we heard a knock at the back door, he sent Stephie out to distribute baby clothes to some First Nations women. We were already part of the ministry. Later, Ibb would come every Saturday morning to teach art to students at the school, bringing his own art supplies.

After tea, Stephie and I walked up the slight hill toward our new school, passing two big white buildings with red roofs along the way. One was marked "Hudson's Bay Company," the other "Indian Agency Office." The school itself was a substantial new three-storey building, white with green trim, and with a portico at the entrance. The top floor had thirteen windows, I counted. It was quite an impressive structure. The school grounds were encircled by a wire fence.

Stephie and I found the principal's office, where we stopped to say hello to the gentleman who had hired us, Reverend Ken McLeod, and met his striking Aboriginal secretary, Elsie Poker. From there we set out to explore the school. The floors were covered in green battleship linoleum, and the school smelled of fresh paint. The four classrooms at either end of the main floor were bright and pleasant, with a row of windows that opened inward. Mother would like this, I thought. She believed in fresh air coming into a room, even in the middle of winter. Every pupil's desk had a boxy drawer on the side and an inkwell. The classrooms met with our approval, each containing bookshelves, a mounted pencil sharpener, a fine teacher's desk, a black chalkboard with red, white and blue chalk brushes and a clock.

Stephie and I were to share a bedroom on the third floor. It was at the end of the hall, across from a shiny bathroom and next to a kitchenette. The room was simple—two single beds with matching bedspreads, two closets and two dressers.

Our last round of exploring took us to the bare children's dormitories on the second floor with their rows of metal beds; then back to the main floor to view the large assembly hall, which had a stage and a piano; and finally downstairs to see the staff dining room, the kitchen, the children's stark dining room and two empty playrooms, one at either end. It had been a long day, and Stephie and I were definitely ready for bed in a much larger "ship" that didn't rock gently or smell of fresh lake breezes.

Chapter 4 🪶

Florence's Story: A Star Is Born

Stephie met Edward Gamblin before the school officially opened that year, since some of the students, including those from Cross Lake, Edward's home community, had arrived early. She'd been asked to help out with some of the younger students, and in one of the classrooms she noticed the smallest boy and spoke to him. He had his pant legs turned up and a rope for a belt.

"What's your name?"

"Edward."

"How old are you?"

"Five."

Stephie gathered some magazines and sat down with Edward to look through them. She'd point to a photo and say simple words like "table," "window," "chair." Edward would repeat the words quickly, then turn the page himself to find more pictures. Stephie realized that he was a little boy who was smart, capable and eager to learn. Over the course of that week, a grade 3 student from Norway House, Marvin Chubb, took chalk down to one of the children's playrooms and taught Edward his numbers and then how to add and subtract.

Each day more students arrived in Norway House by plane, since September 1 was drawing near. The school supervisors and the matron, Miss McClary, looked after them, first showering them in a big washroom four or five at a time. It got so hot and steamy in there that the staff wore bathing suits. The process must have been alarming for children from trappers' cabins who had never even seen running water. Their hair was cut the same way, straight and short. (I wouldn't learn until much later that hair is sacred to Cree people. They do not cut it, and each time they braid it, they say special prayers.) Some of the children had head lice, so all were checked and dealt with accordingly. Both boys and girls were issued jeans, checked shirts and running shoes. Any personal items or clothing were boxed away.

The teachers—Miss Finnson, grade 1; Mr. Johnson, grade 2; me, grade 3; and Stephie, grades 4–7—busied ourselves unpacking school supplies: scribblers, pencils, erasers, straight pens, ink and textbooks. There were no library books that I remember, just the books we had each brought ourselves. I decorated my classroom with large pictures of birds painted by Allan Brooks, taken from a calendar backed with cardboard. I still have those pictures:

The boys of Norway House. Edward is standing third from the left with his pant legs rolled up.

One of the first pictures taken at the new school at Norway House in September 1954. Reverend Ibbs Avery stands to the left in the back row and Ken McLeod is beside him. About half of the boys in this picture are Sayisi Dené, or Chipewyan and the other boys are Cree. Caleb Wilson is in the front row on the far left.

horned lark, robin, ring-necked pheasant, whippoorwill, wood duck, rufous-sided towhée, hermit thrush and white-breasted nuthatch. I would let students have the pictures at their desks when we were doing art, and they took great care of them. They had a master, Mr. Brooks, to emulate.

When September 1 arrived, we all gathered in the assembly hall, boys sitting on one side and girls on the other, arranged according to age. Looking back, I realize that the children were never allowed to sit in family groups. It was cruel, to be able to see your little brother or sister at the school but not be allowed to talk to them. There was no talking of any kind in assembly.

Reverend McLeod welcomed everyone. He was a soft-spoken, gentle man with a warm smile. I knew that he had been a United Church minister for one year in God's Lake Narrows, an isolated First Nations community, and then at James Evans United Church

Edward is the second from the left in the front row, his best friend Raymond McKay is to his left. Christopher Ross, Albert Ross, Alex Crate and Ray Spencer (L-R) are in the back row.

in Norway House. When the school opened, the Department of Indian Affairs designated him as principal, though he was reluctant to accept since he had no formal teacher training. Mr. McLeod read a passage from the Bible, and then we sang "O Canada."

When the assembly was over, the students followed the teachers to their respective classrooms. My grade 3s ranged in age from eight to fourteen. Some were Cree, some Saulteaux; others we knew as Chipewyan, though I would learn later that these people called themselves Sayisi Dené. The Sayisi Dené children were generally older. Some of them had lived out on the Barrens at Duck Lake, north of Churchill, and had not started school until they were nine or ten years old. They had first attended residential school in Prince Albert, Saskatchewan, but since that school was being renovated, they'd been sent to Norway House for the year. They all were timid, quiet and shy—frightened, no doubt, like most children on the first day of school, but even more so.

Reverend McLeod welcomes students and teachers to the United Church Indian Residential School in Norway House.

The rest of my students came from God's Lake, Nelson House, Island Lake, Split Lake, Gillam on the Hudson Bay Railway line, Cross Lake and Oxford House. Several lived right in Norway House and could see their homes from the classroom windows. These children often had parents who were away on the traplines for long periods, or they were orphaned, living with extended families. Sometimes the families of the local children would visit on Saturdays, sitting out front with them in the hall. That must have been hard on the students who never had visitors.

Many of my students were very artistic, and as a group they excelled at abstract subjects like mathematics. By the time I'd written a column of numbers stretching from the top of the board to the bottom and drawn a line under them, many of the children already had the answer. They also enjoyed a game I created of finding places on a map of Canada. I loved nature study myself, so I would take my students out to collect leaves and plants. Then we'd press and identify them.

One day I took my class for a long walk through the autumn forest out to a spot called the Mountain. They had such a happy time, skipping, running and chattering to each other. We all enjoyed the trail through the friendly spruce, sometimes highlighted by a few spectacular golden leaves drifting down. The gentle warmth of the sun and the crisp fresh air invigorated us.

Lorraine Finnson was Edward's favourite teacher

The Mountain was an open space of raised grey rocks with a view of azure blue Little Playgreen Lake. We stopped to admire the scenery once we got there, and then I announced that the students could have fifteen minutes of free time. Every single one disappeared into the surrounding forest. I stood alone in the silence at the top of the Mountain, alarmed. What if they didn't

The girls at Norway House in 1954. The tall girl at the back is Isabel Ross. Her little sister, Rosalie, is on her left.

37

Caleb Wilson was in Florence's grade 3 class. He was a very talented artist.

The children helped Florence make the costumes for the Christmas concert in 1954. The clowns were a big hit, both with the children and the audience.

come back when I called them? I contemplated returning to the school to report to my principal that I had lost my entire class. But I called only once, and they all reappeared. How they must have loved that familiar freedom in the woods.

My class was very discerning. I wondered if that was because they'd been trained by their parents to be observant for safety and hunting purposes. One student, Caleb Wilson, age eight, from Norway House, was outstanding. He was a handsome boy who sat in a front-row seat, and one day after I read the story aloud he drew with crayons a wonderful picture of Snow White and the Seven Dwarfs. In the background were purple snow-capped peaks with the sun's rays illuminating the tallest mountain. A great black eagle flew over a charming house that reminded me of Caleb's. From the window, Snow White peered out. The seven dwarfs walked purposefully down a broadening trail, each dressed differently, carrying various mining tools. On the opposite side was the witch, carrying her basket of poisoned

Mr. Johnson prepared a skit for the boys in which he dressed them up in "Indian" costumes. Edward danced and whooped for the audience. He was born to be a performer.

apples, birds, foxes, flowers and insects. There was even a spider's web on one small tree. Such detail, colour and charm!

The fall went by quickly, and before I knew it, it was December. I set myself a huge task for the Christmas concert: I would make costumes for the Seven Dwarfs. They were designed as clown suits, with ruffles around the wrists and ankles and a big stiffened ruffle around the neck. I used flour sacking for the suits and bought red cotton at the Hudson's Bay store for the ruffles. The students drew big polka dots on the suits and coloured them with crayons. Across each backside their names were printed in black crayon: Happy, Grumpy, Sneezy, Sleepy, Doc, Bashful and Dopey. At the end of their performance onstage, the seven students turned their backs to the audience and bowed. They were a hit. I'd also made crepe-paper skirts for all the girls in my class and taught them a country dance.

And a star was born at that first Christmas concert in 1954. Mr. Johnson had dressed the smallest boy up like an "Indian,"

Edward performed in two skits at the Christmas concert in 1954. In the second skit he pretended to be a boxer who took down three older boys.

poster paint on his tiny bare chest, painted cardboard feathers attached to a headband and crepe-paper fringes down his pant legs. This diminutive boy was Edward Gamblin, and out he went onstage, arms above his head, dancing, stepping high, spinning around, a big smile on his face, whooping and hollering. He brought down the house. The Mountie in the front row laughed so hard he nearly fell off his chair.

"That sure brought the reserve in!" Edward would comment to me years later.

Edward performed in another skit at the concert, too, dressed in a shirt, pants and boxing gloves. He pretended to knock three big boys down. He was a born performer.

As for my life outside of teaching, I was a wide-eyed nineteen-year-old, ready for any new experience. One evening, Joan McIvor, a friendly Cree woman of my age who worked at the school as kitchen staff, asked me if I'd like to go down to the band hall with her to a dance. Well, of course: the entry under

Florence loved to dance and play the piano.

my grade 12 picture in the high school yearbook had read, "Florence Pockett loves dancing."

I decided to wear my Black Watch tartan kilt with its big safety pin clasp and a sheer blue nylon blouse I had made in my grade 12 sewing class. I was very good at sewing, and this blouse had a row of horizontal pleats all across the front. I completed my ensemble with a navy blazer.

Joan and I strolled together across the common, past the Indian Agent's imposing house, past the Hudson's Bay store and down the gentle hill to a dilapidated log structure. The door to the hall was barely hanging on its hinges, and from inside you could see daylight through the log walls, since most of the chinking was gone. There was a hard-packed dirt floor with a few benches along the sides.

The building might have looked down and out, but its occupants certainly weren't. The place was crowded with handsome, young black-haired Cree men and only a few women, plus a vigorous fiddle player and a drummer. Joan said these young fellows

Stephie and Florence standing outside the church.

were just in from their traplines, very ready for a dance and a good time. I was the only white person.

Whoopee! Every dance was a round dance with the left-right chain and swing your partner. I had to be quick-witted when a strong gentleman swung me around enthusiastically, and then we were off again, leather shoes and moccasins flying. I enjoyed the heat, the rhythmic beat, the excitement. The dust began to rise, and the tempo seemed to quicken. Swing your partner, allemande left, and on and on.

Eventually Joan and I spun out the door and headed back in the dark to the school. Whom did I meet on the front steps but my first-ever principal, the Reverend Ken McLeod? My tartan kilt was on backwards, my stunning blue blouse was hanging out from under my navy blazer, my legs were grimy up to the knees and my cheeks were rosy.

The principal smiled. "It looks like you've been having a good time," he remarked.

43

Chapter 5 🖋

Florence's Story: Sniffling and Tiny Sobs

There were approximately 120 students at the Norway House residential school that first year, and only two supervisors. So, early on, Reverend McLeod asked the teachers if we would take on some after-school duties. One of these was to preside over the students' evening meal once a week. The students lined up to file into the dining room, which consisted of long tables and benches set in amongst the basement pillars, girls on one side, boys on the other. As supervisors, we had little to do: we just walked around. In addition, I was asked to supervise in the playroom and then the student dormitory from 6 p.m. to 10 p.m. one night a week. I tried gamely to maintain order.

The basement was a cement box with high windows along one side. There were no puzzles, cards or games in the playroom. There was not even a bench to sit on, just a set of metal lockers along the back entranceway. The area had just one bathroom with three flush toilets. On my shift, I was left alone to supervise sixty girls ranging in age from five to sixteen. How could three toilets stand up to sixty girls? It would have helped if I'd been a plumber! The group included Cree and Chipewyan girls whose families had been traditional enemies for generations, and sometimes a hair-pulling fight would break out. Somehow, we survived till bedtime.

Upstairs, the dormitory was divided into two parts—the

larger section for the juniors, and the other for the seniors. The beds, covered in grey blankets, were set up in rows, and there was no place by the bed for anything personal. No pictures on the walls. The little room for the supervisor in the dormitory had a window with curtains.

Once everyone had washed up, brushed their teeth, changed into pyjamas and scrambled into bed, I sat on a stool to read them bedtime stories. Sometimes I heard sniffling and tiny sobs coming from somewhere in this "far-from-home" place. How the children in those single little beds must have missed their families. And how it would have helped them to have been able to snuggle into bed with a big sister or cousin. They never would have slept all alone in their families' trappers' cabins. There they would have slept on the floor, on sweet-smelling spruce boughs covered with tanned furs, close to their parents' bed. I didn't know this until many years later, though, when Edward talked of this painful, lonely experience to me.

Edward's cousin, Helen Ross, enjoying a book at her desk. The classroom was where the children often felt the safest.

The children had brothers, sisters and cousins at the school, but rarely had a chance to visit with each other outside of the classroom.

Brothers and sisters never had a chance to talk to each other unless they were in the same class. They saw each other only from a distance, in assembly, in the dining room or at church. Not to be able to run over to be with a family member must have been torture. But this was the way residential schools were run. Familial contact was discouraged, often forbidden. Why didn't I think of this at Norway House? Why didn't I make arrangements with the other teachers to have little brothers and sisters visit back and forth in the classrooms for family activities, drawing, reading or acting once or twice a week? Having Chipewyan and Cree children teach each other their customs and languages in groups might have cut down on the fights the children got into outside.

All around the school, Saturdays were spent cleaning—a form of child labour. I always had many volunteers to help me wash and wax my classroom floor. Luckily we had an electric waxer. Cleaning the classroom was the teacher's responsibility.

The students were dressed in uncomfortable and foreign clothing for Sunday school. Edward is on the far left in the front row.

Sunday must have been a terrible day for the students. First they were dressed in good clothes, then they lined up single file and walked across the common to the James Evans United Church, where they were made to sit silently throughout the entire adult service in English, with not even a special song or story for them. Then, again in single file, they walked back to the school, where they had Sunday school in the afternoon. All of the teaching was Christian; there was no mention of the Creator or the rich spiritualism of their people. I was expected to teach Sunday school, which I did. Looking back, I wish I had played active games with the children and taught them some songs with Moses or Joshua in them instead.

Stephie and I both found our once-a-week supervision job overwhelming, especially after teaching all day, so we decided to double up for two nights a week instead. This worked better; one of us could man the toilets while the other thought of some games

47

to play. Stephie was wonderful with the older girls who just wanted to talk. But eventually twice a week on top of our teaching was impossible, so we told Reverend McLeod we could not continue. He agreed and hired more staff for supervision after school.

It was many years before I'd learn what the children at Norway House school suffered, unbeknownst to me and the other teachers. Children were being slapped for speaking their own language, kicked if they didn't line up properly. Most horribly, many were sexually, physically and emotionally abused by a few staff members. Their behaviour set fear into each child's heart. None of them knew what bad thing might happen at any time. It was through reuniting with Edward and other students that I would later learn all of this.

Chapter 6 ✒

Edward's Story: Scenario That Never Left

I was born on May 17, 1948, in Cross Lake, Manitoba, to Wilfred Roscoe Gamblin and Jane Mary Gamblin (née Sinclair).

My father was from Norway House. He died on November 20, 2005. My mother was from Cross Lake, and we lost her to a vehicle accident in Winnipeg in 1975. Their union was headed for separation from day one of their marriage. In our Cree culture, forced marriages were rituals adhered to by our grandparents, and the men who showed a good work ethic were the ones my grandpa, Albert Sinclair, chose as life partners for his daughters.

I was given the names James Edward Albert Gamblin after my grandfathers, James Gamlin and Albert Sinclair. I should explain: my full-blooded English grandfather's last name was "Gamlin." It was later, when Indian Affairs was registering the Natives, that the "b" was added to the name. My grandfather was from Breckenhead, on the west coast of England. He worked cutting wood at Pine Falls and apparently sent money via men going to Norway House to give to my grandmother. But the money never arrived, and their relationship ended. At first, I fought against this English ancestry, but eventually I accepted it.

The union between Wilfred and Jane Mary was in trouble. My parents were not in love, and they certainly lacked the skills to provide care and comfort to a newborn baby. Those first years our little family lived in Wabowden, Manitoba, where Dad had been working. The family at the time consisted of Mom and Dad, my younger sister, Joyce, and me. Many times I'd see Dad cranking away on this old thing from which beautiful music would blare. It turned out the person we were listening to was none other than Hank Williams, Sr. I remember playing on the floor with those big black disks. In the centre, which was yellow, there was a picture of a dog looking intently into a long cylinder. These, I later learned, were records, and Dad had a large collection of various artists.

It seems that those first years after I started into this life's journey, someone had mapped it all out for me. Around every bend, hidden pain was ready to spring up and hit me squarely where it hurt the most. The scenario that has never left, and the one that lies like an animal in the dark of my brain, as if waiting to attack its prey, is one that never ceases to tear my unsuspecting heart into shreds. It's my first recollection of life. I am about a year old, and I'm crying, standing on the deck of our house. It is quite high, and I'm holding onto the pant leg of my uncle Eric for support. I believe he had been visiting us. We're standing up on this deck, and we're watching my dad beating up on my mom on the ground below. She is crying and begging my dad to stop. My uncle is only about ten years old, too young to go to the aid of my mom. My dad is drunk. He is yelling and shouting, and he keeps hitting my mom, who is crying and bleeding. *Damn!* This scene used to be so painful when it would come on. During those first two years at the residential school, this sickening scene would replay itself. I'd be lying in bed in the dark, sniffling and trying my darndest not to make too loud a noise, and I would recall this episode. Most Sacred Spirit, why this torment? Why? Wasn't it enough that I had to commence my walk through this hell from an early age?

Unbelievably, even so, I'm still thankful I ended up at a foster placement at Cross Lake. I guess there had been a verbal agreement between my parents and the old couple, Mr. and Mrs. Sandy Monias. I learned from my foster brother, Donald, that I arrived at their house when I was two years old. My foster father wasn't at home most of the time. He'd be out hunting or doing other traditional things that needed doing for us to survive. When I grew older, I was never too far behind him. I was either walking as fast as I could or running to keep up with him. I was so in love with my foster dad, and the reason was, he showed me how much he loved me by the little things he'd do. He was so active, and such a hard worker. He would give me things to do, and I'd try hard to do them right so I could get praise from him. Every August, my foster dad and my older foster brother, Fred, and I would be out most of the month. My foster dad had a barge and an old eight-horsepower outboard motor we used to haul hay and the winter supply of wood. When he and Fred were shouldering the logs down to the barge, he'd set aside small ones for me to take. This made me feel so proud, to be helping with the work.

My older foster sisters, Saline Apetagon and the late Jean McKay, were my moms during my baby years. Their chore was to change me and keep me fed. I heard from my other sister, Verna Hamilton, that the girls would fight over who would get to pamper me. I can't remember the years between two and five years old, but from stories Verna told me, I guess I came along and took over the house.

Those summers at my foster home were so exciting and fun, and my foster family was so loving. The traditional teachings and the principles and values I learned from my foster mom and dad, I still hold today. Yes, these I will treasure until my last breath.

From Florence:

Edward told me once how his biological father, Wilfred, in a drunken rage, chased his mother and him with an axe. In his song "Cross Lake Rain," the cold rain is a metaphor for pain. However, someone had also mapped out for Edward, around every bend, opportunities to discover his God-given talent as a songwriter and a musician. Those big black disks of Hank Williams Sr.'s music entered his very being, awakening a gift that brought him satisfaction, great happiness and fame as a recording artist.

Cross Lake Rain

Standing here it all comes back again
The years come rushing back down on me.
I remember how hard it used to be
It used to be so cold, the Cross Lake rain.

Through it all mama always smilin'
I can hear little Joycie cryin' again
I can see her tears slowly fallin' down
Mixing slowly with the Cross Lake rain.

Chorus:
The rains kept comin' on and on
Lord it seemed like there was no end.
Albert Sinclair bin in touch
There ain't no way I'll trust this Cross Lake rain

Didn't have much but her faith was strong
In the night I'd hear her softly prayin'
But she'd watch her dreams come crashing down.
Getting washed away by the Cross Lake rain.

Chorus repeats

(Edward Gamblin—Cree Road)

Chapter 7 🖋

Edward's Story: My Mind Goes Back

"My mind goes back to days I wish I had not known. Guess these vivid pictures that lay silent for so long will be etched in memory 'til I'm lowered into the ground. One question that cuts a clean painful trail to the soul, Oh, dear Lord! Why do I have to keep feeling, thinkin'? Somehow..."

It was such a devastating and ugly experience. I remember that day crystal clearly. I stood there, my legs and insides shaking, staring at this humungous monstrosity in front of me. It amazes me, when I look back, that a five-year-old kid didn't collapse out of sheer fright. Worse, that time I had no loving hand or pant leg to hold onto for support. My Father, Most Sacred Spirit, where were you? Even today...do I have a right to question? That residential school building was the biggest structure in the world to me. To a five-year-old, no other existed.

Looking back fifty years, that picture still causes a painful bleeding from my heart. I wonder why the motive to end my life has never crept into my tortured mind. My buddies, my friends, fellow residential school survivors who took that route—will the burden of taking their own lives fall strictly on them, for committing the act? I know the act would never have been executed if that sick, assimilative process hadn't been passed in Parliament by perverted, supposedly honourable members of the domineering federal government of Canada.

That night I was asleep in the school dormitory, in dreamland, playing with Mervin and Zachius in the front yard of my foster dad's residence, laughing and having fun, when I was suddenly yanked up and thrown against the edge of the metal-framed structure that passed for a bed. Over me stood my tormentor, Mr. S., one of those the United Church had hired to provide care. That sacred responsibility had been given by the Creator to Wilfred and Jane Mary Gamblin, then transferred to Sandy and Adele Monias verbally, in a Native adoption agreement. Yet now this monster was beside my bed against the red exit light hanging in the junior dorm, giving him an eerie outline in the dark. *My Father, my Protector, Creator, I need your help!* Mr. S. leaned over and so softly whispered in my ear, "You cry out, and I'll take you downstairs where no one will hear you, and you'll get the strapping of your savage, meaningless little life!" *Mom? Mom?*

I saw him lifting his hand and I waited for that familiar pain. It came like the times before, with the ringing that followed. *My Lord, what did I do to deserve this?* Then my tormentor ordered, "Say the Lord's Prayer, and you better not make any mistakes."

Lord, honest—I really tried. My goodness! But what did he expect from a five-year-old who hadn't mastered English, a foreign language?

And then, like before, that KICK! I somehow managed to get back up. But I kept making mistakes, and the slaps, kicks and hits kept coming. This carried on for about fifteen minutes.

Mom? Mom?

Suddenly, I was alone. I crawled back into bed and pulled the covers over me, trying hard to stifle my sobs. Pictures of my foster parents went through my brain, bringing on salty, silent tears that rolled down my cheeks. It was so hard to stop them.

The more I thought of home, the more I cried.

Then, through the thin grey blanket I saw a light. It wasn't like the fluorescent lights that were used in the dorms. Ever so slowly, I lifted up the corner of the blanket and snuck a peek. There, on the next bed, sat a smiling man encircled in a bright blue light. He had black hair and a beard. His hands were palms up in his lap. There was a hole in each hand with blood trickling from it. Imagine the fright I felt. I tossed the covers back over my head and, through the blanket, watched the light slowly fade.

Finally, I somehow mustered enough courage to come out from under the covers. Silently, I got down on the floor and started crawling. I knew my cousin Christopher's bed was at the other end of the dorm. When I found Chris, he was sleeping with his face turned toward the window. I slipped under the covers with him and fell into a deep sleep right away.

It must have been a dream, but it came on like a movie. Everything was so vivid, so clear. I could see my foot touch the windowsill. I looked up, and I was standing at the bottom of these shimmering stairs made of gold. Blue lights were pulsating all around. It was an awesome sight. I started climbing at a snail's pace, a step at a time. I savoured the feeling of comfort that quietly wrapped itself around me. Every step was more comforting than the one before. It seemed like forever. For some unexplainable reason, my five-year-old thinking knew I was in a sacred dimension.

Then, suddenly, I noticed a figure in a cloak standing at the top of the stairs. I couldn't make out his face, but this strange apparition emitted a comforting aura. The closer I got, the more a feeling of exhilarated bliss and warmth took over my being from within. He spoke to me as I ascended the last flight of stairs. He spoke in English, but somehow I was able to understand every word he said. Ever so gently, he told me, "You cannot come any farther. You have to go back."

I started crying. The thought of returning to that place of hell, that place where every day we were faced head-on with some kind of abuse, terrified me. Reluctantly, I turned and started back down the stairs. With each downward step, the feeling of being unwanted returned. I was going back to a place of strict rules and regulations, where there was no love or respect. My tears just kept spilling out.

When my foot hit the windowsill, I was jerked out of my dream. It was my cousin Chris, poking me in the ribs and saying I had to return to my bed or we'd all get a strapping if I was caught in there with him.

That first year at the residential school, 1954–55, is a blur for the most part. There were approximately forty boys from five years old to sixteen. There was an influx of boys and girls who had been brought in from the Churchill area. These kids were of Chipewyan descent. These boys made up more than 50 percent of the male population. It was the same on the girls' side. I recall on numerous Saturday and Sunday mornings we'd play a game we called "war." It was played by two teams. One side was made up strictly of the Chipewyan kids and at the other end were the Cree kids. On our side there were boys from Cross Lake, Gillam, The Pas, Oxford House, Nelson House, God's Lake, Norway House and Island Lake. We young ones didn't really look forward to this game.

I learned to fight the first year at school, when I was five. Even if I was down on my back, I knew I had to scratch, spit, whatever, but never give up, never walk away, or they would never leave me alone. Those Chipewyan boys were mean and threw hard punches.

The food we were fed three times a day was most times not fit for human consumption. To make things worse, they served it on plastic plates and in tumblers that lacked colour. The food was already cold by the time we filed into the dining room area, said grace and sat down. Bread was stacked, one slice per student, in the middle of the table. Always, before we started eating, our "table captain," an older boy who had reached senior status, would point to one of us little boys, and we would have to sneak out bread or another item for him after the meal was over. In the playroom there were steel lockers along the walls where the senior boys had a pillow case, and this is where we'd

Edward at Norway House with his kindergarten report card.

dump the food we had snuck out of the dining room.

What I remember of the time I spent in the school is that I was continuously hungry. We boys—Raymond, Sidney and myself, I recall—we snuck into the reserve at night and begged for bannock from our relatives. So many times, when we would play with the boys who came into class from the reserve, they would tell us how envious they were of us because we had three meals a day at the residential school. Wow! If they had only known.

As soon as we stepped inside that school every September, they took away our freedom. We were given numbers instead of names and locked up at night in our respective dormitories.

The prime reserve land transferred to the Church from the federal government was fenced off around the residential school.

Edward and the other children were always hungry at the residential school. At night they would sneak home and beg for food from their families.

If we snuck past the fence, we were severely punished, at times receiving the strap on our hands, but mainly bent over on a chair and whipped on the bare bum. The other boys were forced to watch. During these strappings and whippings, the boys' supervisor would yell profanities and make derogatory remarks about our racial background. His remarks were always about our elders and our parents being savages and about them being ignorant.

For years after I had left the school, I was ashamed of who I was and of my culture. I looked down on the elders and other members of my community.

Chapter 8 🖋

Florence's Story: Peter and Shirley

The end of June 1955 eventually arrived, and it was time for the children to leave. They were dressed in new clothes provided by the school, and they looked happy and excited. They were flown home to anxiously waiting parents, brothers, sisters and grandparents. The Gillam and Churchill children were flown to Wabowden, where they boarded the train north, escorted by two teachers, Lorraine Osterlund and Keith Johnson. Local students were picked up by their parents. Edward was flown home to his foster parents at Cross Lake. I took a picture of him dressed in his new clothes, holding his first report card.

I too went home for the summer, and I returned to teach at Norway House the following year. A new boy named Walter sat in the front seat in my classroom. All he ever wrote down was the date and title of the work from the board. I never understood why, but thinking back, I realize he probably needed glasses. Not one of my students in those first two years had glasses. I never saw a public health nurse who checked the children, and a dentist came to the school only once in three years, to my knowledge. He just pulled out any decayed teeth and sent the child back with a tissue and a little paper cup to finish bleeding in the classroom. I remember a boy named Peter asking, horrified, "Are they going to pull some of my good teeth? I have no cavities!"

That year flu broke out in the crowded dormitories, and some cases turned to pneumonia. Every child except one, I believe, came down with sickness, plus more than half the staff. The doctor from the hospital came up, but no extra help was flown in from Winnipeg. One hundred and nineteen children with flu and pneumonia! The staff who lasted were exhausted. Theresa Robicheau, the senior class teacher, was exceptional. When the last child had recovered she came upstairs and said, "I'm tired. I think I'll have a rest."

Theresa was loved by her senior class, grades 4–7. Her students always gathered around her at recess and after school, wanting to talk to her. The first day of school in September, when she asked her class to follow her to the classroom from the assembly hall, was usually the last we saw or heard from them. Her students were always quiet like her, attentive, happy and well behaved.

After Florence's first year of teaching she went home for the summer, but returned again the next year.

The third year I was at Norway House, 1957–58, Shirley Robinson from Ontario was the grade 1 teacher. She believed children could not read a language until they could speak it, so she spent many months playing with her students, doing crafts, games and singing.

One boy from God's River, Peter, was disabled, having a withered arm and leg from polio. Shirley insisted that Peter do as much as he could for himself, and she would not let other students help him. Peter would get down on the floor and hold the paper with his knee, doing his best to cut out whatever he needed. Shirley knew life was going to be hard for him, and, wisely, she wanted him to learn to do as much as possible for himself.

The school inspector, Mr. Marcoux, came into Shirley's class and reprimanded her for not having her students read from the grade 1 readers, which featured Dick and Jane. In case he came back again, she had the students put the readers on their desks. Finally, about March, when she felt they were ready, Shirley had the children turn to their readers. They soon could read fluently, with pleasure and comprehension. She was an expert teacher.

The winters in Norway House were particularly beautiful. I snowshoed along trails lined with snow-laden inky spruce as snowflakes drifted soundlessly down. You could hear the silence. It was as if a person or a spirit was communicating with you, and you'd strain your ears to hear. Sometimes the tinkle of dogsled bells could be heard far behind. Jack, who worked at the Hudson's Bay store, advised me then to "get right off the trail and let them pass, or the dogs will go for you."

The northern lights, the crunch of snow under my mukluks, the moonlight on the snow and the brilliant stars. Beauty. As I looked out my third-floor window one morning, the sky was sapphire blue, and the branches of the trees over by the Indian Agency were decorated with thick hoarfrost, each colour bouncing off the other.

The winter was very long in 1955, with the ice continually melting and then freezing over again. After eight weeks, our small community was running out of everything. We hadn't had any mail for ages. One morning we heard a big Expeditor plane fly over. "Maybe they'll drop some bags of mail," Stephie said. No; hay for the horses. We were disgusted. At last the ice began to break up. We could hear it cracking, grinding and groaning. As we watched from the second floor of the school one morning, great slabs of ice heaved and ran over each other and eventually travelled down the Nelson River current to the end of the lake. Miraculously, in just a few hours, the ice was gone.

The next day—great exhilaration! Bags and bags of mail were dumped in the front hall of the school. Looking back, I wonder if there were any letters for the children in those bags, or did they have to listen to the excited, laughing adults?

Suddenly, it was spring: the caw of a crow, the whistle of a chickadee and the almost imperceptible sound of water dripping from the icicles as they eased their tenacious grip on the eaves. The trickle of an infant stream began to talk. Before long, bare patches of ground showed tiny green blades of grass, then a dandelion or two. Off came our fur-lined parkas and warm mitts.

The northern lights were always a thrill in Norway House, but particularly in the spring and fall. The other teachers and I would climb out the big window at the end of the second-floor hall and step out onto the composite roof—against every rule—to see them better. From there, we marvelled at the swooping, swirling yellows, greens and pinks of the aurora borealis. They captivated us for as long as they lasted, sometimes only minutes, sometimes hours. At times they moved up and down, like curtains on a stage.

One night, a group of us went down to the hospital to watch a movie with off-duty staff members there. When I became bored and restless, I went out onto the deck, and from there I beheld a great green V of northern lights as it began at the zenith and spread out and down to the jagged horizon of dark pointed spruce. The awe-inspiring vision was reflected in the lake, too, making it feel as if the lights were moving up to engulf me.

Very often, Norway House days ended with spectacular sunsets. As the sun dropped slowly behind the dramatic spruce-laden islands, dazzling multicoloured clouds sang in the sky. Green, gold, mauve, apricot and red filled the semicircle to the apex.

Then, imperceptibly, the colours slid across the still waters of Little Playgreen Lake and were reflected back in the windows of James Evans Memorial Church on the point. There was a hush as the palette slowly faded and the first star of the evening appeared. We were blessed many times by the Creator's breath-taking sunsets.

In late 1956 a new staff member arrived to take up the position of school nurse. We heard she was coming all the way from Scotland; her name was Fiona. One fine day she arrived on the *Chickama*. Those of us watching at the front door were taken aback when a woman burst in the door, all out of breath and looking furtively behind her. After she calmed down, we asked, "What is the problem? What is your name?"

In a broad Scottish brogue, the woman announced she was Fiona, the new nurse. "Is it safe here?" she demanded. "My mother was horrified when I told her where I was going to get a job among Indians, but I was willing to take the risk for adventure away from my staid community at home."

We all liked Fiona, especially me, because she looked after me when I had jaundice. She never went back to Scotland, as far as I know, because the next year, when I left to teach in Winnipeg, she married a local Cree man and moved away from Norway House. I wondered what her mother thought of that.

Chapter 9

Florence's Story: The Strap

After teaching for a year in Winnipeg, I returned to Norway House in 1957–58 as head teacher. I had forty-four Cree students of various ages. They were all from central Manitoba, places such as Island Lake, The Pas and Cross Lake. Their desks completely filled the room, so we had very little opportunity for extra activities. They were very quiet, well-behaved students, partly because they were still working at mastering English, white culture and the religion taught at Norway House. It was difficult to truly bond with individuals in this overcrowded classroom.

Edward was in my class that year. He was eight years old and in grade 3.

One incident outside the classroom that year haunts me to this day. It was a Saturday morning. I was cleaning up my bedroom, which was above the boys' dormitory, when I heard *whack*! *whack*! *whack*! *whack*! A pause, and then again, *whack*! *whack*! *whack*! I stood stock-still, listening. It sounded like some boy was getting a terrible strapping. I wondered if I should go down. I wished my roommate, Lorraine, were with me. We could've gone down together. But there on my own, I did nothing.

Years later, when I was visiting Edward in the Health Sciences Centre in Winnipeg, he told me, "One Saturday morning, I ran innocently upstairs to get something out of my locker in the dormitory. When I pulled the door open, there was my supervisor, Mr. J., having sex on the floor with a teacher. He scrambled up and pulled up his pants, obviously raging with anger to be caught, interrupted and embarrassed. He came for me and grabbed me, pulled me into his office, yanked out a strap, pushed up my sleeves and viciously, repeatedly strapped me on both of my wrists. The shock and pain were excruciating. I backed away and fled to the playroom. Both wrists became very swollen, with black and blue welts so painful that for days friends had to feed me."

"Why did Mr. J. strap you on your wrists?" I asked Edward.

"He knew I would cover up the marks by pulling down my sleeves."

The memory of the sounds I had heard that long-ago Saturday morning flooded back. Trembling, I told Edward, "I am sorry. Perhaps that was you getting strapped and tortured. I should have run down the stairs to investigate."

"It wouldn't have made any difference," Edward responded.

When I told my sister Lorna about this despicable episode, she said those injuries could have caused permanent damage to Edward's circulation. I feel sick to my stomach and my throat tightens as I write this now. I look at Edward's photograph in its silver frame and cry. To think those students had no one to turn to, no official advocates at the Norway House Residential School.

In 2010, while I was visiting Edward in Norway House, he started to tell me about the sexual abuse he experienced at the hands of the supervisor Mr. S. in 1954–55.

"Mr. S. would take me into his supervisor's room, with the curtains pulled shut but his light on," Edward said. "He would always have me lie on his bed on my side with my face to the wall, where I had to watch Mr. S.'s shadow while he worked his penis."

Edward could not continue the story from there, and he changed the subject.

Later, while going through her father's papers after he died, Edward's daughter, Angelique, found Edward's written account of this episode. She cried as she told me about it. After reading it, she said, she tore the paper into a thousand pieces, burned them and then sobbed and sobbed.

Edward also told me about an incident when Mr. S. took the boys down to the lake to swim. Even though Edward could not swim, Mr. S. threw him in the water. Then Mr. S. repeatedly held his head under water. I suppose Mr. S. did this to keep Edward terrified of him, so he wouldn't tell anyone about the abuse. There is no telling how many times or in what ways Mr. S. sexually abused Edward.

A progression of other supervisors at the residential schools sexually assaulted Edward later, one at age twelve and another when Edward was fourteen. These perverted men were never charged but were shipped out to other schools. The children were afraid to speak up about these criminals. They were afraid of losing the good staff who would report the incidents if they told. Edward thought at the time he was the only one, but the man who had assaulted him when he was fourteen was later found abusing five little boys. Edward related all of this to me fifty years later, when we became friends. How devastated he must have felt, thinking he was the only one.

"The school supervisor was feared like the devil; teachers like Kaefer were on the side of the angels," Richard Wright wrote in the story on Edward and me published in the *United Church Observer* in May 2009. "This distinction, says Gamblin, led the children to devise strategies for survival. For example, it was a sadistic trick of the supervisor to tell the children as they set out for class what punishments they could expect when they returned at the end of their classes. 'You had to live in fear of that all day,' says Gamblin. 'So we'd deliberately act up in class so we'd get a detention, so we didn't have to go back to the residence right away. The only places that were safe were the classrooms.'"

Edward told me, "I have forgiven these men for what they did to me, and I would go to see them, but they are all dead now."

This must be the ultimate in forgiveness, another reason I respected and loved him so. Forgiveness was Edward's path to healing.

Chapter 10 🖋

Edward's Story: Freedom and Prison

Religion was an essential part of the curriculum throughout grades 4–8 when I attended the Norway House Residential School. The United Church minister at the time would come in and teach us about Christian ideals and values and other moral principles surrounding biblical teachings.

Most of those teachings I had learned from my foster parents. They were avid churchgoers, and of course I had to go as well. Sundays at my foster placement in Cross Lake were taken in reverence, and many were the Sunday evenings the United Church minister would conduct home services in our residence.

But during the ten months out of each year we spent at the school, we were treated no better than caged animals. This treatment was dished out by those hired by the United Church— supervisors who carried out their duties and responsibilities overzealously. Yes, many of them were nice, but those were the ones who didn't last long and most times transferred to other schools. I remember one very understanding individual, Mr. Brian Rowden, who treated us with respect. All of us boys liked him, but I guess those in authority noticed that he was too kind. It wasn't long before we found out he had been relocated to another school in Manitoba. Another one was Mr. Ken Crassweller. We young ones would romp around on the floor with him. We'd gang up on

The teachers at Norway House. The students loved Mr. Ken Crassweller (middle).

him, and when he was able to get free, he'd chase us around the playroom. Mr. Crassweller didn't last long as a supervisor and was assigned to teaching. At least we didn't lose him. We were still able to interact with him on weekends and holidays.

Not wanting to lose those people we liked and trusted, we kept what we experienced (the sexual and physical abuses) from them. We knew that if we told them about the abuses, they would try and do something to stop what was happening. We would then lose them, because those in authority didn't want the sacred name of the Church defaced.

I witnessed the torture and abuse a disabled student named Peter went through. He suffered at the hands of a fellow student. The puzzling thing was, the supervisor let these things happen right in front of him. The student had some homemade darts with a pin sticking out in front. He would force Peter to run in a circle down in the dungeon (our name for the playroom), and this big boy would throw the projectiles at Peter as he ran by. We were forced by the other big boys to watch this abuse. Peter would have five or six darts sticking out of his back. It sure hurts thinking back on that, seeing Peter running by, crying, with those things sticking into him. Many years later, I phoned the lawyer I had used for my residential school settlement and gave him Peter's address and phone number. I also told the lawyer I was willing to relate what I had seen.

I left Norway House Residential School after grade 8, at age fourteen, to attend the United Church Indian Residential School in Portage la Prairie.

From the beginning, it was very noticeable that the administration and the staff in the residence of the residential school favoured the southern Indian students over us kids coming in from northern Manitoba. If things happened around the school— if items were missing, or there was vandalism on school property—the northern "savages" were to blame. Many were the times fights broke out between the Anishinabe (Ojibway, Oji-Cree and Saulteaux) boys and the Cree. Of course, it was the Cree students who'd get the finger pointed at them, and those in authority always believed the allegations. All of this was difficult to adjust to.

However, one positive activity was the choir at the Portage school, which I joined. I was asked to sing alto because I could harmonize. Some boys would have been embarrassed by that, but, being musical, I accepted. The choir travelled to various communities, including Winnipeg, in a bus with the words *The Singing Indians* painted on it.

It was a typical autumn day, 1964. I was sixteen and had barely made it into grade 10. This was my second year at the provincial school in town, the Portage Collegiate, where I never experienced racism. We Indians were legally allowed to quit school at age six-teen. When I went back to the residence after school, I asked my supervisor, "May I go now?"

"Yes."

However, that supervisor tried to encourage me to stay in school because I was so bright and talented. Through frustration, he even threatened to hit me. But a big friend of mine, John Hart, was standing nearby. He threatened the supervisor, and the man backed off.

I walked out the front steps of the residence, spread my arms in the air like an eagle and proclaimed, "I am free." I had earned my freedom, freedom to feel whatever I felt, without the fear of reprisal, be it physical, sexual, emotional, mental or spiri-tual abuse. I sobbed and sobbed. Then my protective friend and I, with just three dollars between us, set off to hitchhike along the Trans-Canada Highway, toward Winnipeg and the unknown.

Part of the unknown turned out to be trying to survive on the tough streets of north Winnipeg. One day I was walking down the street minding my own business when a white fellow about my age started teasing and taunting me, highlighting my race. He wagged his finger above his head to imitate feathers, then put his hand to his mouth and "war whooped," making sounds of an Indi-an dancer. Bent at the hips, he pranced around me.

No longer could I take this humiliation, so I went for the white fellow. The tormentor took off. I was an extremely fast run-ner. (I would actually have won the provincial half-mile in Portage to try out for the Olympics, but instead I'd gone behind the school before the race to smoke up. I lost that race by half a second.) That day I caught up with my tormentor and followed him into his house and pounded and beat him up. His parents phoned the police. No questions asked when the police arrived—I was Indian. I was taken to the Stony Mountain Penitentiary. I served my time there and felt it wasn't so bad. The food was better than at the residential school I had just left.

When I was released, I went home to Norway House for a while. Eventually I found life there too slow and boring, but while I was there I wrote some songs, and I formed a band called Cree Nation in 1966 with three local boys. The song called "Running on the Wrong Side" expressed my feelings.

Seen many times she cried
Cursed my old man the night she died
Lord I took a little run down the road
Ain't no use hangin' around
Burning inside.

Chorus:
Just a fool on the run
Runnin', runnin' on the wrong side
Started running with the wrong side
Lord I got by pushin' and a poppin' them highs
Oh there's guilt, the skills to survive
Lord I got on with a girl with faraway eyes

Chorus repeats

Went home a couple years back
Rossville didn't suit me
It seemed a little too slow
Little sister she's doing all right
There's nothing she needs. I just had to go.

I need a bit of looking back
And what I've done I wouldn't want my mama to see
Somehow I took the wrong track
Somehow I turned out far from
What she wanted me to be.

Chorus:
Just a fool trying to hide
Runnin', runnin' on the wrong side
Oh yes runnin' on the wrong side.

(Edward Gamblin, *Classics 1984–1986*)

But I felt I needed more excitement, more involvement, so I moved back to the tough streets of north Winnipeg. Drugs, booze and trouble were easy to find. Once I stole a case of hard liquor and was arrested again. This time I was handcuffed to a murderer and returned to the same place—Stony Mountain Penitentiary, a gigantic, grey, looming monster of a building perched on a great hill. The second time in this dungeon, regardless of the food, I decided this situation was not for me, and I was never arrested again.

Chapter 11

Florence's Story: Going Back

I left Norway House in 1958 and taught at Murdoch Day School on the Fisher River Reserve for the next two years. Then I moved to Alberni, BC (now part of Port Alberni). Teaching First Nations children at the United Church Indian Residential School in Alberni was a different experience. These grade 2s were not shy or withdrawn. Students at this school had been forced to speak English for several generations, and the first day I couldn't get a word in edgewise or get the children to sit down. So, I changed my teaching style. I enjoyed four years with the students there, from 1960 to 1964.

I didn't understand the implications at the time of all those children speaking English. Much later, I would come across a quote from Randy Fred, a Tseshaht writer and publisher who is a survivor of the residential school in Alberni where I taught. Fred's father spoke to him only in English when Fred was growing up, to save his son from persecution. "The elimination of language has always been a primary stage in a process of cultural genocide. This was the primary function of the residential school. My father, who attended Alberni Indian Residential School for four years in the twenties, was physically tortured by his teachers for speaking Tseshaht: they pushed sewing needles through his tongue, a routine punishment for language offenders."[1]

I also met my future husband, Gerd Kaefer, in Alberni. We married in 1962. Gerd came to work as a boys' supervisor at the school for a short time, and then worked as a bus driver. We lived in a teacherage up on a hill above the red brick school. My job took up most of my time, so I knew little of what went on in the main building where the dormitories, playroom and dining rooms were located.

I did have one incident when a little boy came back after lunch, crying. I asked the other boys what was wrong. They said Mr. Plint had boxed the boy's ears, which were very red. I went over to the main building and confronted Mr. Plint. As he stared at me with cold, extremely dark eyes, I told him never to touch my little student again. Of course, he paid no attention to me.

It was many years before I learned of the terrible sexual and physical abuse of children at the Port Alberni school, in particular by this supervisor, Arthur Henry Plint, who was later sentenced for his actions to twelve years in prison with no chance of parole.

In 1998, in a courtroom in Nanaimo, BC, Willie Blackwater, Randy Fred and thirty other former students filed a civil lawsuit that also named as abusers both the federal government, which was responsible for the legislation governing residential schools, and the United Church of Canada, which ran the school in Alberni.

When the brutality and sexual violence of the residential schools was exposed, I was horrified. I became reluctant to even tell anyone I had taught at the schools in Norway House and Alberni. By then, I was teaching in a public school in Courtenay, BC, and I also had children of my own, born in 1967 and 1969. I began thinking, what if people of another culture were to come and take my sons by force at age five or six? I could understand more completely then how First Nations parents and grandparents must have felt.

I stayed home with my boys until the younger one, Ian, started kindergarten in 1974. For a while after that I taught part time, taking courses and graduating from the University of Victoria with a degree in elementary education in 1987. I continued to teach in Courtenay, retiring in 1995. My husband graduated from the University of British Columbia with a degree in elementary education as well, and he became an exceptional teacher himself.

I lost my beloved husband in June 2004 to cancer. Two years later, my sister Lorna's daughter, Barbara Grexton, a teacher, extended an invitation for me to take a road trip with her and her mother to Churchill. "We could make a side trip down to Norway House, where you taught at the United Church Indian Residential School," Barbara said. I gladly accepted.

In preparation for this trip, I packed the two albums of photographs I'd taken during my years in Norway House. Some people had suggested I send these to the United Church Archives, but I knew I'd much rather return them to my students, if I should happen to meet any during my visit. I also took along the portfolio of student art that I'd saved from my Norway House years. I planned to return the artwork to the school and offer to pay for it to be framed. Barbara made arrangements through the principal for me to visit the new school there, the Helen Betty Osborne Ininiw Education Resource Centre. The school was named after a young Cree woman, a grade 12 student from Norway House, who was brutally beaten and then murdered in The Pas in 1971. Four men, white locals, were implicated in her murder, though due to a botched investigation, only one of them was ever convicted.

Lorna, Barbara, my sister Kae, her husband, Don, and I set off on our journey from Grandview, Manitoba, on July 18, 2006, heading north on Highway 83 to The Pas. At first we drove through gently rolling land, lovely with its yellow canola fields, patches of evergreens and birch and distant views of farm buildings. Past

Swan River, the countryside grew very flat, with masses of tall magenta fireweed standing brilliant against dark swamp spruce. We had beautiful sunny weather as we approached Dawson Bay, one of the innumerable bays of Lake Winnipegosis. The lake's name means "little muddy waters" in Cree, and the salt flats, reeds and many wildflowers beckoned us to stop. We inhaled the fresh breezes blowing off the lake and listened to the waves tumbling onto the shore. Not a sign of habitation or other travellers, except for two pelicans heading for the lake. Reluctantly, we got back into our car and drove to The Pas.

The Pas is French for the Cree word "pasquia," which means "wooded narrows." Until 1912, this settlement was called Paskoyac, for the Opaskwayak Cree people who still live there. We visited the town museum, which had drawers full of intricate First Nations bead and quill work. Next morning, leaving The Pas, we crossed a huge railway bridge spanning the mighty Saskatchewan River, a river that begins as a trickle of water on Alberta's gigantic Columbia Icefield, and eventually flows into Hudson Bay.

We drove north of The Pas, turning east at Simonhouse onto Highway 39. We stopped for lunch at a service station and restaurant called Ponton, and when I went up to the cashier's desk I noticed one lonely CD left on a rack. The cover was black with white lettering: "Edward Gamblin." The name rang a bell. I asked the cashier where Edward was from and how old he'd be. "Cross Lake and Norway House," she replied. "He's about fifty." I wondered if he could be a former student of mine, so I purchased the CD.

After we left Ponton, we headed south toward Norway House on Highway 373. About halfway there, we came to a huge dam and generating station called Jenpeg. Years ago I had read an article in *Equinox* magazine about the damage done by the dam on the Nelson River in 1979 to Cree traditional lands, about the social problems the dam had caused and the outright lack of respect for the environment. We took a break here and looked way down to the Nelson River, where a flock of pelicans was fishing. We drove on.

Eventually we came again to the Nelson River, where we boarded the C.F. *James Apetagon*, which can carry only two or three vehicles at a time. Once across, around a bend in the road, we soon saw a remarkable "Welcome to Norway House" sign. A blue construction painted to simulate waves was mounted on a giant rock also painted blue. Behind this was a huge York boat, with four figures on board rowing with long oars, a figure in the bow watching the course ahead and another steering at the stern. Behind the boat stood another large sign announcing "Norway House Cree Nation." Extending from one side of the sign was a flag depicting a V of flying Canada geese, and at the base of the blue rock were painted black bears and a large moose.

As we drove into Rossville, a part of Norway House, I didn't recognize a single building or marker. I was bewildered. We continued down strange roads until, off in the distance, I saw the familiar outline of the James Evans Memorial Church out on the point. We walked down to the church after supper. It was boarded up, its paint peeling, looking forlorn. People had gathered on shore to watch the huge red and black York boats out on the lake. The rowers were preparing for the upcoming York boat races to be held during Treaty Days in early August.

The first York boat, built in 1749, was named after the HBC trading post at York Factory. Aboriginal rowers had travelled hundreds of miles in these boats, laden with furs, making long, arduous portages around rapids and waterfalls. They were paid in tea, flour and sugar.

As we sat in our car by the shore, I commented to the woman in the truck beside us on what a beautiful evening it was. When

I told her I'd taught here in 1954, and that my name used to be Florence Pockett, she was surprised, and so was I—the woman was René Paupanekis. René's family had lived in Norway House for many generations and her grandfather was William Paupanekis. He was the first Swampy Cree to be baptized by Reverend James Evans in Norway House in 1842. He became a church leader. "C'mon," René said. "I'll take you down to my place." I'd hardly said goodbye to my family when we were off.

René's beautiful modern house was beside the old house where we used to go for church services with her gracious parents, Esther and Max. We'd travel with either Reverend Ken McLeod or Reverend Ibbs Avery, by boat or Bombardier. Their small house could warmly enclose at least six of us. I always thought of the Bible verse Matthew 18:20: "For where two or three are gathered together in my name, there am I in the midst of them."

René and I walked down to the river, to the spot where our boat used to pull in. The view was so peaceful. Back inside, she showed me pictures of her parents and a photograph of her mother rocking her baby in a traditional cradle, taken by Theresa Robicheau, that had appeared in a United Church calendar. When René drove me back to our motel, she stopped briefly at the hospital where she works.

The next day, through René, I was invited to walk down to Stella Muswagon's house. I'd taught her in 1954. She was sitting on her porch in a wheelchair, and we were excited to see each other again. When I told her during our conversation that I hiked with a group of friends, sometimes covering twelve or fourteen kilometres, Stella replied, "I once walked three hundred miles from here to Winnipeg with a group, protesting the failure of the law to charge the four white men who viciously murdered Helen Betty Osborne." It was their protest that had finally achieved a conviction, and I was proud of her.

Later that day I visited two more friends: Olive Flett, René's sister, was the current United Church minister in the community, and Gloria York had been one of the students in my 1954 class. Gloria had seven children she'd raised on her own after her husband died, she told me. She said what she'd learned in residential school had helped her do this. Several of Gloria's children were now teachers, and Gloria herself had become a United Church minister. She had no hard feelings about residential school, she said, and I was glad to hear this. Two of her grandsons were at the new school in Norway House, and they were both accomplished violinists.

The next morning, I took my photographs and the portfolio of student artwork over to the new school. It was summertime, so the teachers and the principal weren't there, but the school maintenance staff were all very interested in the photographs, recognizing various people in them and telling me where they were today.

I showed the school staff several paintings done by Caleb Wilson before we embarked on a tour of the new school. There was a huge gymnasium, a fine library, a music room, a woodworking shop, a hairdressing classroom and more. At the end of each hallway was a painting by Norway House artist Gayle Sinclair evoking the culture, spirit and beauty of the community. While I was on the school tour, someone had phoned Caleb Wilson's granddaughter, Jackie Wilson. Caleb was off sturgeon fishing at Molson Lake, she said, but she'd be happy to come and get his pictures. I gladly gave them to her. For one picture, I had asked the class to use a single colour of paint. Caleb had chosen green, with which he had painted three distant snow-capped mountains, a few green slashes for clouds, two small eagles in the distance, a huge mountain in the foreground from whose peak burst forth a gigantic eagle with outstretched wings and finally a gentle curved slope in the corner, like a hilltop from which to view this magnificent scene. The other painting was of a man—Caleb's father,

Florence was grateful for the opportunity to meet Jackie, Caleb Wilson's granddaughter. Jackie happily accepted his painting of the dog sled.

I guessed—driving his dog team, with a fir tree in the foreground, the lake nearby and the man's tiny house in the distance, with the sun shining on it. Caleb had added shadows in the appropriate places, too. What a gifted artist, and a homesick one. I took a picture of Caleb's granddaughter holding his dogsled painting and gave her a photograph of Caleb in 1954, sitting at his desk with another of his paintings.

The following morning we left Norway House Cree Nation. I was sad to leave it behind. It was a changed community in many ways, with good roads, bridges and an exceptional school.

After returning from Churchill and Thompson, we stopped for lunch at a fine restaurant called My Place, where I found another Edward Gamblin CD called *Cree Road.* After we'd checked into the hotel in The Pas, I opened Edward's CD and read the liner notes. I was shocked to read the words, "From the age of five until he was sixteen years old, Edward Gamblin was an unwilling captive of the residential school system in Norway House and Portage La Prairie, Manitoba. Fifty-three years later, Edward received the first of his financial compensations for physical and sexual abuse at the hands of the Church and State-run facilities." I began to cry, telling Lorna and Barbara what I'd discovered. I said,

"I can never think about teaching at Norway House in the same way again." Eventually, I fell into a troubled sleep.

The next morning, as we drove, Barbara suggested we play Edward's CD on her car stereo. "No, I cannot listen to it," I replied. I was still too upset about what I'd learned.

It wasn't until I arrived home in Courtenay a few weeks later that I read the rest of the liner notes for *Cree Road.* "Though this [the financial compensation] has helped Edward on his healing journey by allowing him to better look after himself and his family, he still awaits the elusive 'We're sorry!' The 'We're sorry' the survivors so badly needed to hear from the people who perpetrated these crimes against the children and their families. Here's to the hope that one day soon we as a country can start to heal... together!" The liner notes also said that Edward had been sober for twenty-seven years.

Finally, I worked up the courage to play Edward's CD. His song "Survivor's Voice" began with a sound that reminded me of the wind whistling and howling around the residential school at the end of the third-floor hall in winter. Next came Edward's voice, saying, "Her words cut like a knife when she asked, 'How come you never say you love me, daddy?'" And then he sang.

At five years old they tore me up inside
Took away my innocence, poured holy water on me
They took my soul and placed it at the foot of their cross
Took me down forbidden fields late at night

Eleven long years...still haunting me
Look close enough you can see the pain in my eyes
With calculated skill they took away who I am
Then they filled my innocent head with strange white lies

Could never understand why you can't look at me
The fire I walked through wasn't my choice
Why just me...Canada heal with me!
Open your heart you'll hear a Survivor's voice.

The next verse, in Cree, was followed by:

You called it a sin...called down my people's wheel
Started to believe, started thinkin' it was real
With calculated skill you took away who I am
You cut away the cord then you taught me not to feel

Could never understand why you can't look at me
The fire I walked through wasn't my choice
Why just me...Canada heal with me!
Open your heart you'll hear a Survivor's voice.

(Edward Gamblin, *Cree Road*)

On the back cover of *Cree Road* was a picture of Edward, leaning against a building in a blue shirt and jeans, an orange Harley-Davidson cap and dark glasses. His hair was tied back, and he had his hands in his pockets, his guitar slung over his shoulder.

At the bottom of the back cover were two phone numbers. I dialled one of the numbers, and Rick Roschuk answered. When I explained who I was, he said, "You may speak to Edward yourself on his cell."

My heart skipped a beat as I dialled the number Rick had given me. The phone rang, and a man answered.

"Edward speaking."

My heart skipped another few beats.

"This is Florence Kaefer. I used to be Florence Pockett. I was in Norway House recently and bought two of your CDs."

"You are one of the ones I remember," Edward said. "You were my teacher."

"I just love your songs. They make me dance," I said.

Edward laughed, and then I began to cry. It took me a moment to gather myself. "I'm so sorry for the terrible things that happened to you in the schools."

"Where are you calling from?" Edward asked.

"Vancouver Island. Do you remember dressing up like an Indian and dancing in the school concert?" I asked.

"That sure brought the reserve in!" Edward replied. "I would like to stand in front of my teachers now and thank them for encouraging me to stay in school. My executive producer, Rick, and I are planning a healing circle, and you are the sort of person we would like to have in it."

I was too overcome to speak—overwhelmed, joyous and deeply touched. When Edward said farewell in Cree, I did my best to repeat the words.

The next day I phoned Rick Roschuk again. He referred to me as "my dear lady." Edward had called Rick to say that talking to me had moved his heart to a happier place, Rick told me. He said he'd never before seen Edward respond positively when anything about residential schools was mentioned.

I hung up, again filled with joy. I hoped Edward hadn't been offended by anything I said. We were just getting to know each other again. I'd already decided to offer him my help in finding any other teachers or supervisors he wished to contact for his healing circle.

Chapter 12 🪶

Florence's Story: Finding Edward's Teachers

The first teacher I contacted at Edward's request was Marion Mars, now Marion Ogibowski. We had kept in contact over the years, mostly through Christmas cards. When I phoned her and related Edward's story of many years of abuse, Marion was dismayed. She had gone to work there when the school opened, and she truly loved the children. Marion had been very energetic, young, always smiling and confident. She'd unfailingly done her best to find fun activities for her boisterous little charges. She'd taken them frog hunting, wading or swimming, ending by washing them up and tucking them into bed. But Marion had talked to some of us about the worries she had back then. She suspected wrongdoing on the part of the senior boys' supervisor, though she could never catch him at it. Now I gave her Edward's phone number, so she could phone and talk to him. He told me later how wonderful it was to talk to Marion.

Edward and I continued to speak on the phone regularly, and he told me his favourite teacher had been his first one, Miss Finnson. Lorraine was gentle and smiling, an excellent teacher. "I remember having to stay after school banging away on an old piano," Edward told me, "with Miss Finnson trying to work at her desk. Years later, it hit me. Miss Finnson must've suspected that I was bothered by something that was happening on the other side of the building. I was unable to disclose the shame I was subjected to, but I guess this was the reason why she'd make me stay in class. I used to dread it when detention was over. God bless her soul!"

Lorraine Finnson had only stayed at Norway House for one year, and I hadn't kept in touch with her. I remembered that she was from the Interlake area, though, perhaps Gypsumville, and after many dead ends, I located someone who knew her husband, Ken Warren. Ken told me Lorraine had suffered from severe arthritis and had passed away a few years earlier. She'd often spoken fondly of Norway House, he told me, and they had returned there one summer. Ken said he would be very pleased to meet Edward. If Mr. Gamblin was ever passing by on his way to Winnipeg, Ken said, he should come by for a visit. Ken sounded as genuine and as special as his wife had been.

Over the years, I had kept in touch with Ken and Lesley Crassweller, who had since moved to Victoria. Edward was overjoyed to be back in contact with Ken, his favourite supervisor from Norway House, and they began a renewed friendship by email. With more detective work, I was also able to reconnect Edward with Keith Johnson, a kind and caring teacher ahead of his time who had tried to make his classroom feel like a home with curtains he'd made himself, a carpet, vases of dried flowers and a tall lamp. He did many activities with the boys, who appreciated him. My former students always asked about Mr. Johnson. I gave Edward Keith's phone number. He phoned, and the two of them talked briefly.

Ruby House had been another outstanding teacher at Norway House, a woman from Newfoundland who was a beautiful singer, an excellent piano player and a devout Christian. I'd visited her once in the intervening years and been treated to her wonderful Newfoundland hospitality. Ruby was very upset to learn

Ken Crassweller and Avery Ibbs. Edward reunited with Ken, his favourite supervisor from Norway House, and they began a renewed friendship by email.

about the abuse Edward and other children had been subjected to. She contacted Edward and invited him to come and visit her.

Edward's grade 8 teacher had been Verna Kirkness, a Cree woman from Manitoba, who subsequently became a famous First Nations educator and was responsible for establishing the First Nations House of Learning at the University of British Columbia. Verna had always encouraged Edward to set his educational goals high, and when I contacted her in 2010 to let her know Edward was in hospital in Winnipeg, she went to see him. They joked and reminisced together, Edward told me afterwards.

There were many more teachers Edward mentioned whom I hadn't been able to find, so I had an idea. I put an ad in the *United Church Observer* asking any teachers who remembered Edward Gamblin from the United Church residential schools in Manitoba to contact me. Several more did.

A stunning poster arrived in the mail that December. Edward had designed it himself to promote his song "Survivor's Voice." In the upper left-hand corner of the poster was a black and white photograph of Edward as a very young boy, being held by his mother. Below, printed on a rust-coloured strip, were the words to the song. Below that was a Creator's wheel—yellow, red, black and white. Highlighted in the middle of the poster was an Aboriginal boy, his dark eyes questioning. Tears fell from one eye, gradually changing in size from tiny to large. Joining the last tear was a small maple leaf, followed by larger and larger leaves that finally dropped out of the frame.

One afternoon Edward phoned me from Edmonton, where he was employed as a healer for Aboriginal girls who lived on the street and struggled with drugs such as crystal meth and alcohol. He was on his break, so he could talk for a while. He told me he also did healing circles and sweat lodges with troubled people. One woman had come all the way from Ontario to have him conduct a sweat lodge ceremony for her. His routine was to work in Edmonton for a month, then go home to Norway House for a week.

We talked about his family. Edward had been married to Aurelia Monias for thirty-two years. He wrote a song to honour her called "You're My Everything." "I never could have done the things I did without her... Aurelia suffered a serious aneurysm in 1996," he told me. "She still has problems with her speech, but she is slowly recovering. We have five children. We've had trouble in our life together: we lost a twelve-year-old boy. He killed himself. Losing our son Virgil was very hard. We have three daughters, Candida, Angelique and Jane, and another son, Vernon. We also have an adopted son, Jared. Our granddaughters, Cree-Anne and Daija, are so beautiful and fun to play with."

I'd learned that *Cree Road* had been nominated for Best Album of the Year by the Aboriginal Peoples Choice Music Awards, and I congratulated Edward on that. He laughed. Then he said, "My break is over, and I'd better put some soup on for my girls. Mequetch."

After we hung up, I listened to "You're My Everything," the song that Edward had written for Aurelia. The lyrics touched me deeply:

It's your smile that always gets to me
When you too start trembling inside
Your warm touch just drives me crazy baby
I can't wait to see you tonight.

You're my everything, the air I breathe
You're the one that reaches deep inside
Ain't no one can hold a candle to you
I can't wait to hold you tonight.

Chorus:
Don't know what I'd do without you
Beautiful lady you're my everything
Without you, girl, my world would end
Beautiful lady you're my everything.

It's those little things that get to me
They get to tremblin' deep down inside
When I touch you I get an awesome feeling
I can't wait to see you tonight.

(Edward Gamblin, *Cree Road*)

In subsequent calls and emails, Edward told me more about Virgil, the son he and Aurelia had lost to suicide. Edward had written several songs in memory of Virgil. He was very aware of the high rate of suicide among Aboriginal young people, and he hoped his songs might save someone from the pain he and Aurelia had suffered. In one of these songs, "Your Name on a Cross," he sings about Virgil while his guitar screams with pain.

> Another young eagle just learning how to fly
> We watched your dream wash away in the pouring rain
> Swinging in the wind, dangling at the end of the line
> Nobody heard his call to ease the pain.
>
> A line of cars headin' for the dying fields
> Toward the west you can hear an eagle cry
> Watch the young dreams get buried in the ground
> It touches the soul to hear a mother cry.
>
> *Chorus:*
> You'll be leaving behind things that they don't want
> Broken hearts, mother holding your shame
> All that's left, picked flowers on the ground
> Your name on the cross fading in the rain.
>
> Hey young friend don't be afraid to call
> You hold your people's future in your hand
> Don't look down—hold the feather high
> Face toward the east. Pray where you stand.

(Edward Gamblin, *Classics 1984–2008*, volume 2)

Chapter 13 🖋

Florence's Story: Time and Distance

Edward and I corresponded regularly, and on April 16, 2007, I received the following letter.

> Ms. Kaefer,
> Sorry I haven't responded until now. It sure has been a busy spring what with Winter Carnivals, etc. happening in northern communities. Our band Cree Road has been to about 6 communities entertaining and it sure ain't as easy as it used to be. I'm feeling my age I guess! The family is ok and healthy. My wife Aurelia still hasn't commenced on her speech therapy. It sure is frustrating how Medicare can take so long in coming. (This therapy <u>must</u> be done very soon after an aneurysm or the patient never recovers speech.) Anyway, the girls are very supportive and always there when she needs assistance. That is really nice to see.
>
> My three daughters live with us along with two of the youngest daughters' girls and our boy Jared. It sure is nice to be able to interact with our kids and it brings the family closer together. Problem is overcrowding? What problem? We love it!

'Til next time, may the Creator and the Grandfathers stay close.

Ekosi (later),
Edward Gamblin

Later that month I received an invitation to my fifty-third
Normal School Reunion, to be held in Winnipeg in June. Stephie
phoned from Nova Scotia to say she was going and encouraged
me to come, too. I agreed, suggesting we go visit Edward in Norway House after the reunion.

A month later, I learned that Edward was in St. Boniface
General Hospital, across the Red River from Winnipeg. He had
blocked arteries in his leg, and doctors had found something
under his stomach.

I was worried about Edward. I prayed for him and listened to his music. I learned from his friend and executive
producer, Rick Roschuk, that Edward's family had come down
to be with him because he had to have an angioplasty. There
were some risks, but if all went well, he would be home by the
weekend.

Edward had his operation, and it seemed to clear the block-
age. The doctor could not be absolutely certain, but he told Edward
his ulcerated leg should also heal. Once Edward was home to rest
and recover, we kept in touch by email and phone. He was eager
to have Stephie and me visit in June. He would hold the healing
circle he had dreamed of then. He was also excited that we'd be
able to meet his wife, Aurelia, and his sister Joyce, who he said
had a thousand questions for us. "Geez—it must be over 50 years
since we last saw each other in person. Wow!" he wrote in one
email. When the day to leave Winnipeg arrived, Stephie and I
packed up to head north.

We were excited, too. At the Perimeter Air terminal, we climbed into a sleek, green-trimmed white aircraft that seated about twenty people. We taxied out on the runway, and then with a huge roar we were up and flying over the outskirts of Winnipeg. Soon, far below us, we spotted large white pelicans silhouetted against the electric blue water of Lake Winnipeg, heading north. To the east spread miles of undisturbed forest.

There was no one to meet us at the small terminal in Norway House. I knew it was a long way to the York Boat Inn, where we'd booked a room. But luckily we met two teachers from the new school who were picking someone else up, and they offered us a ride. Stephie and I were both thrilled to see the northern landscape again: the Nelson River, Little Playgreen Lake, the dark muskeg, the spruce and tamarack trees. A feeling of breathless anticipation arose in me. This was Edward Gamblin's territory, a place of beauty and of hardship, too. I could scarcely wait to meet him again in person. The little boy I had known fifty years ago was a famous recording artist now.

The next morning, a bluish-grey double-cab Chevy truck with running boards pulled up to the front entrance of the motel, where Stephie and I stood waiting. A small man with a grey moustache and long grey hair stepped out. He wore glasses, a black leather jacket and a cap. He walked with a slight limp. Stephie held back a bit as Edward and I smiled, then hugged each other.

"I wish I had hugged and comforted you long ago, when you were a little boy and needed someone to care," I told him. In that moment, years and distance vanished.

Edward visited at the Inn with us for a while. I showed him my photograph album of Norway House, bringing back memories, perhaps haunting ones for him. Then he politely said his family was waiting for us, so off we went. As we drove down the road to his place, dust flew out behind us.

Inside his charming, bright home we met Jared and Edward's sister Joyce. His wife Aurelia gave us a beautiful smile, but she couldn't speak. Edward showed us pictures of Aurelia's mother and sisters and of Aurelia as a young woman. Then he served us Oreo cookies and tea. Edward announced that the healing circle would be held in two days' time. He wished a few more teachers had been able to come. As he spoke about some of the tortures he had experienced in residential school, tears came to his eyes. But later, as Stephie joked about some of the things she had done during her only year at Norway House, Edward responded with an infectious laugh.

Edward joined Stephie and me for supper at the café across the common that evening. He and Stephie chatted easily while I leaned in close to hear his every word. He told us his biological parents had been severely affected by alcohol, but that his mother was the sweetest, most wonderful person when she was sober. He added, "Sometimes I used to go home and help her clean her house, wash clothes and cook for my brothers and sisters." Edward wrote a song called "She's Finally Goin' Home" for his mother's funeral in 1975. He'd deposited tobacco on her grave, he said, leaving the pain she had caused him there.

He found deep healing in the sweat lodge, he told us. "The heated stones are the Grandfathers—angels," he said. "One shone so brightly I was able to find my inner child." He was grateful for what he had learned from the Moniases, the family who'd adopted him when he was two.

I inquired about some of my former students. Two brothers had drowned, Edward told me, and so many of the others were gone. Edward recalled how a boy named Andrew had hated him in school, picked on him, beaten him up and made him a slave. All I could remember of Andrew was that he was in the senior class, played guitar and was a fine singer. But eventually Andrew became a glazier, Edward continued. He suffered injuries in the job. Badly cut up, he was down and out. He came to see Edward and asked him for some money. Edward had given Andrew two hundred dollars, and now they were okay.

The story revealed Edward's character, I felt—forgiving and generous.

Chapter 14 🪶

Florence's Story: The Healing Circle

Edward did manage to contact a few of my former students, and the next day, a Sunday, I joined him at the café to meet them. Edward stood up to wave Stephie and me over, and there at the table were Christopher Ross, Leonard Ross and Raymond McKay, along with Edward's sisters Joyce and Joan and his wife, Aurelia. We drank coffee, talked and laughed until it was time to go. Edward parted from us with his usual farewell: "Later."

When Edward came to pick us up the next day, I could hardly contain myself. The healing circle both of us had dreamed of was about to happen. As we drove to Edward's place, I sang along with his song playing on the truck's stereo, "Runnin' Down the Road."

Soon we arrived again at his sunlit, love-filled home. Family and friends were gathered around the large dining room table. A sweet little granddaughter sat beside her Auntie, who was cutting up fruit into a big bowl. Dazzling light poured into the west window, highlighting the fish tank and filling the entire living room with warmth. On the walls were pictures of family, even a framed one of me standing on the steps of the Helen Betty Osborne school which I had sent to him in the mail, and the children's art was posted on the fridge. The beautiful, large oak table and matching chairs seemed to speak of family discussions and good times. Beside the computer and stereo was the matching china cabinet, filled with delicate cups and saucers and varied treasures. At the far end of the living room were a big comfortable chair, a couch and a wide-screen television set.

First Edward introduced us to his three daughters, Candida, Angelique and Jane, his youngest, and to his granddaughters Daija and Cree-Anne. After some conversation, the house grew quiet. The children disappeared, and a few more adults arrived. Christopher Ross, a big sturdy man in glasses and a grey cap, carried a drum. Leonard Ross, younger than Christopher but no relation, joined us too.

Edward, wearing a red cap, welcomed Stephie and me. As teachers from the residential school we were the day's special guests, whom he wished to thank and honour. Someone put cushions on the living room floor, and Edward invited us all to sit down. Seating himself on a low stool, he placed a wrapped package in front of himself. He carefully undid it, arranging some of the objects inside in a particular order. He then put the rest of the bundle aside. Finally, he positioned a Bible and a large feather. Christopher began to play a soft, steady beat on his drum and to sing in Cree.

Edward filled a small cast iron frying pan with fragments of herb-like plants, each from a separate package. He lit these. They burned for a while, then began to smoulder. The smoke smelled a bit familiar. I'd later learn that the components were tobacco, sage, cedar and sweetgrass. Edward cupped the smoke into his hands and slowly spread it over his hair and face. He took another handful of smoke and directed it over the rest of his body. Christopher then picked up the frying pan and slowly walked around inside the circle, stopping in front of each of us and indicating we were to do what Edward had done. Christopher touched each of our heads and said a quiet prayer, a blessing from the Creator. He used the feather to direct the smoke toward us. Later, Edward would explain to Stephie and me that this was called smudging.

Candida, Edward's oldest daughter, and Angelique's daughter, Daija.

The smoke cleanses you of bad feelings, negative thoughts and evil spirits. This helps healing to come in a clear way, both physically and spiritually.

Next Edward took up his bundle again and lifted out a deerskin bag. Reverently untying it, he withdrew a long peace pipe and held it up for all to see. He loaded the pipe bowl with four ingredients, tapping them down to fill it. He lit the pipe and puffed a few times, causing the smoke to rise above his head. He then held the smoking pipe up to the four directions.

Edward passed the pipe to the person on his left, who puffed on it and then passed it to the next person. I was sitting next to Edward, and I anxiously waited for the pipe to come to me. This was going to be a new, very special, experience for me. Once the pipe had gone around the circle, Edward filled it again, drew on it and spoke words in Cree, and the pipe made its way around once more. In all, the pipe circulated four times.

The healing circle took place in Edward's home. Back row L-R: Christopher Ross, Edward, Leonard Ross. Front row L-R: Stephie, Aurelia, Joyce, Jane and Angelique.

I had a hard time with the pipe. My eyes watered, my throat burned, and I coughed. Too late, someone advised me, "Don't inhale." I had quite a prolonged burning sensation. The last time the pipe came to me, I saw a large, brilliant sun. Its rays extended before my eyes. I couldn't control my emotions. Briefly, I wept. I finally managed to announce, "I just saw a shining sun, and I am honoured to be included in the circle. Edward, you have made my heart happy."

Now the pipe was in Edward's hands. He added more elements, took his cap off, wound his long grey hair back, and puffed on his pipe until the sacred smoke rose above his head in curling swirls, a spiritual presence around him. He spoke to his Creator and to the four directions in his beauteous, melodious Cree. This image of Edward will stay in my mind and heart forever. I knew then how spiritual, cultural and special he was.

Edward's good friend Leonard came and spoke to me after

the ceremony. He talked softly to me about my husband, Gerd, and the loss of his father. Leonard said for me to let Gerd go, and then it wouldn't hurt so much. "You won't forget him," he said, "but you'll be happier and at peace." Edward added, "The beautiful sun was your husband."

Edward's people had smoked the peace pipe with white leaders they trusted when treaties were signed. This was their way of signing and sealing a great, unbreakable promise. I had read about such historic events as a student, but I had never dreamed I would smoke the peace pipe myself in a circle, with First Nations people honouring Stephie and me. What a privilege to be welcomed and trusted in Edward's healing circle.

We were all treated to a feast, including a great bowl of cut-up fresh fruit and Dream Whip, along with the date-filled oatmeal cookies I had bought at Gunn's famous North End Winnipeg bakery.

To add even more to their hospitality, Aurelia and Edward gave Stephie and me decorated bags filled with gifts: two candles in a glass; a feather tied at the ends with red wool and tanned deer hide; a white brocade book with a gold cross on the cover and a glass guardian angel and a verse inside; a tea Thermos; three of Edward's CDs; and freshly woven sweetgrass. Giving gifts is part of Cree culture. Stephie gave Aurelia a small flower pin and told her that she was Edward's flower. Aurelia was very pleased and beamed her special smile.

The next day, Aurelia and Edward took Stephie and me on a tour of Norway House in Edward's blue truck. We stopped at Church Point and the war memorial. We visited the place where the racing York boats were stored, the Children's Head Start building, the Star Daycare Centre, the personal care home and the Kinosao Sipi Minisowin Agency.

I was surprised to discover during our tour that Edward was an accomplished visual artist. At most of the places we visited, he showed us paintings of his, people in traditional garb and pictures of animals central to Cree culture—wolves, loons, bears and horses. There was also Norway House scenery—the lakes, the iconic spruce and the islands. On one wall hung two moose hide shields decorated with red fabric, fur and feathers. But most memorable and touching was a small painting Edward showed us of a little boy dressed in red. The boy was his son Jared.

We stopped in to visit Edward's cousin Albert Ross, who had been a student in Stephie's class in 1954–55. Afterwards, we stopped at Caleb Wilson's house. Caleb was away guiding, but I left his picture of Snow White and the Seven Dwarfs, done so long ago, with his daughter.

The last stop on our tour was the old belled Hudson's Bay Fort gate and the fort's 150-year-old jailhouse with its massive stone walls. Edward related how a First Nations prisoner once held there had changed himself into a bird and flown in and out at will. A shape-shifter!

Back at the York Boat Inn, it was time to say goodbye to our generous hosts. Stephie and I were laden with gifts, and we had been changed and blessed. "I'll be expecting a phone call tonight to let us know you are safely back in Winnipeg," Edward said. "Later." This, I knew, would be a lasting friendship.

Chapter 15

Florence's Story: Aurelia and Edward Come to Visit

Edward wrote that he had returned from a two-night gig in Sandy Bay, northern Saskatchewan, "earning many $$$." He also sold twenty-five CDs in one hour at Fond-du-Lac. He commented that my visit with Stephie had been a wonderful, touching experience. "The children who'd never made it home were with us in that circle," he wrote. "I know the Creator was smiling after that visit." He continued, "I believe the first cheques are going out today to Aboriginal people for the cultural, sexual and physical abuse they suffered in Indian residential schools across the country." When he received his settlement, he said, he wanted to take Aurelia to Edmonton, and then to come out to BC and visit me.

I immediately emailed back to say how pleased I'd be if they came. Finally, a date in early January was chosen. I was excited and honoured that Edward and Aurelia were coming to my house in Courtenay. How to prepare for their arrival? What to serve them? Edward asked if, during their visit, we could go to see Ken Crassweller in Victoria. So we also planned for that.

Their plane arrived early, so I was just in time to see Edward and Aurelia come through the door at the airport. Edward was in a wheelchair, wearing a black and grey checkered cap over his long grey hair and a broad smile. Sweet Aurelia was just behind him.

We hugged and said, "Hello—so wonderful to see you." Then we were off with their luggage and out to my car. Edward was fine to walk short distances, and he stood admiring the mountains for a few minutes.

As they came through my front door, Edward said, "I feel that this house is filled with love." I'd set out my photograph album on my dining room table, open to the page with the picture of Edward at age five, dancing at the 1954 Christmas concert. We were planning to visit Ken Crassweller right away, so he and Aurelia looked through the album while I packed my things. Before long we were on the road to Victoria. Edward was wowed by the great trees and mountains of Vancouver Island. We talked and talked as I drove.

As soon as we'd checked in at our hotel in Victoria, Edward phoned Ken, who said he'd wait outside his apartment block to show us where to park. As soon as we spotted a man at the designated corner, Edward laughed, saying, "That's Ken. He still has that distinctive way of walking."

The two of them were so excited and happy to see each other again after fifty years. Ken's wife, Leslie, was a relaxed, warm person who made us comfortable right away. Ken suggested we go to a nearby restaurant for supper. We all walked over together, though Edward limped.

In 2006, Edward had undergone a five-valve heart bypass operation. Some arteries had been removed from his leg to repair his failing heart, and stents were inserted into his right leg. Then, in May 2007, he'd had angioplasty surgery. In June, after my visit with Stephie to Norway House, he'd written to say he had nagging pain from the angioplasty, but he was sure that it would gradually go away. His right leg had not healed after nearly two years, though. Why not? I was worried.

After dinner, back at Ken and Leslie's place, Edward asked if he could bring in his pipe. He thought that the smoke would

Edward and Aurelia flew out to Vancouver Island to visit Florence. They drove to Victoria so Edward and Aurelia could meet Ken Crassweller and his wife, Leslie.

set off Ken and Leslie's fire alarm, so he decided to just explain the ceremony instead. He started with the four directions, then told us how his foster parents had taught him the seven values of the Creator: Love, Honesty, Courage, Caring, Humility, Wisdom and Truth. The most powerful was Love. Next, Edward opened his bundle and showed us what was inside. The bowl of his pipe was made of red pipestone found deep in the ground in South Dakota, he told us; he'd gone there himself, using a hand trowel to dig down twelve feet through rock to get to the beautiful stone. The wooden stem was made of ash. The two pieces of the pipe were tied with a blue ribbon to keep the medicines to be burned in the pipe in the bowl. Edward's pipe was also beaded with the four sacred colours. He carried it in a bag Aurelia had made for him. On it he had painted mountains, trees and feathers. The mountains represented his spiritual name, Rocky Mountain Man, the trees his children and the two feathers Aurelia and himself.

Edward told Ken about the evening the supervisor had yanked him out of bed and ordered him to say the Lord's Prayer, slapping him around. He described the dream he had had afterwards, after he'd snuck into Christopher's bed, about the bright light, the figure with the outstretched hands and the beautiful staircase he'd climbed.

He'd gone back to school to complete grades 11 and 12 as an adult, Edward explained to Ken, when his children were young and the family was living in Winnipeg. He'd studied literature and poetry, since he knew he wanted to be a songwriter. After Virgil committed suicide, friends had sent Edward for healing sessions in Kentucky. He'd done many different types of jobs before studying at the University of Manitoba to become a social worker. He'd cleared road allowances, done carpentry, mushed with twenty-one dogs and roofed a hospital.

Reminiscing with Ken triggered Edward's emotions, and he began to sob, his head in his hands. I wasn't sure if it was the right thing to do, but I put my arm around him and cried too, saying I was sorry.

He replied, "None of you were to blame. If you had said anything, they would have punished us even more."

After Ken and Leslie had told us some stories about their teaching adventures in the Arctic, it was time to leave. The Gamblins had had a very long day. Edward and his favourite supervisor said an emotional goodbye, and we were soon back to the hotel and in our beds.

The next morning, my phone rang at 6:11. Edward was already up and ready to go. I got dressed quickly, laughing. The three of us drove around Beacon Hill Park, then out to view the Olympic Mountains across the water, which were beautiful in the early morning light. Many seagulls were up already, too, drifting, soaring and squawking.

After breakfast, we went to the provincial museum, where Aurelia purchased some clothes for their granddaughters and Edward bought a silver inukshuk mounted on an Olympic ring to wear on his black suede jacket.

We drove back to Courtenay that evening, and the next morning I saw lights on downstairs around 4 a.m. Edward was probably up, I thought. By the time I came down, Edward had already made coffee and wanted to take Aurelia and me out for breakfast. So off we went to Smitty's for strawberry waffles.

I'd asked Edward if he'd do a healing circle in my home, and he agreed. Late that morning my two sons and their partners and two friends arrived to join us. We gathered upstairs in my living room. I moved the furniture around so that I could make a large circle of cushions. Edward sat on a low blue stool facing east. He conducted the healing ceremony, as he had done in his own home, for all of us present.

How I wished my dear husband, Gerd, had been there with us. He had honoured the First Nations students he worked with at the Alberni residential school, loving them, having fun with them, respecting them. In his beginning prayer after the smudging, Edward said, "All the departed are here with us, those who have gone before." I realized I was sitting on a cushion Gerd's grandmother had embroidered many years earlier, and I heard the wind chimes Gerd had given me jingling sweetly out on the deck. As people spoke, I was touched by how Edward cared for us all.

All too soon, the healing circle had ended, and it was time for Edward and Aurelia to leave. I took a photo of our group on the staircase before we rushed off to get our guests onto their plane.

Sitting in the waiting area, Aurelia looked so relaxed, beautiful and happy. As I hugged the two of them goodbye, I thought again how blessed I was to have them in my life. I waited until I saw them climb the stairs into their plane. Then I went outside and watched the big white bird carry them away.

Sometime later, Edward phoned to say he had had an email from Ken, who'd written that his heart was at peace now. "That is what I wanted to happen for Ken," Edward told me.

Chapter 16 🖋

Florence's Story: Interviewed by CBC Radio

I received a phone call from Cecile Fausak, liaison minister for the United Church residential schools. She had seen my ad in the *United Church Observer* inquiring about any teachers who remembered Edward Gamblin. If Edward agreed, Cecile asked, would I be willing to be interviewed with him on CBC Radio? I said I would.

Edward did agree to the interview, and it was set up for a date in May. Edward was interviewed via telephone from his home in Norway House. I was hooked up to a recording system by the CBC's Michael Tymchuk so I could speak with Edward and Duncan McCue, the interviewer in Vancouver, from my home in Courtenay. The interview ran live on CBC's *The Current* on May 19, 2008.

Duncan McCue is Anishinabe himself, a member of the Georgina Island First Nation in southern Ontario. After asking me some questions about the residential school at Norway House, he asked Edward what it had been like to be contacted by one of his former teachers.

Edward: It was surprising and very emotional, I guess. I'd been trying to connect for years.

Duncan: What did you two say to each other when you talked?

Edward: We just reminisced about the times we were there at the residential school.

Duncan: What was life like for you at the school, Edward?

Edward: It was hell, I guess.

Duncan: Hell. Why?

Edward: There was no freedom. We were locked up, fenced in—numbered.

Duncan: You said on your CD cover that you had been sexually abused at Norway House.

Edward: Yes.

Duncan: What happened?

Edward: Ah, there was a...I'm not sure...So. Yeah...

Duncan: It obviously was not a good experience at the school.

Edward: No.

Duncan: What happened when you left school?

Edward: Nobody prepared me for the freedom I was experiencing out there. It led to things that I regret, like alcohol abuse and the things that come with it.

Duncan: Florence, how did you feel hearing about the troubled times Edward had with alcohol and things like that because of what happened at the residential school?

Florence: It was very difficult to hear. He was such a beautiful little five-year-old boy when he came. To think he had been physically and sexually attacked by a predator was absolutely heartbreaking.

Duncan: Edward, how did you turn your life around? Because you have turned yourself around.

Edward: Yeah. I came from what you call a broken home, where both my parents were alcohol abusers. That's what made me want to change. 'Cause I didn't want my kids to go through the same things I did.

Duncan: You didn't want to pass it on.

Edward: No. I wanted the cycle to break.

Duncan: What role did music play for you?

Edward: I just used it for my addictions at first. But then it became more like therapy that I used when I came out of excessive use of alcohol. Then I started using it as a teaching tool.

Duncan: Florence mentioned a song that you had written that got you two connected.

Edward: What song is this?

Florence: "Survivor's Song."

Edward: "Survivor's Voice." Yes. For the longest time I'd tried to write it, but the feelings would get in the way, and I wouldn't be able to put it down in words.

Duncan: Florence, what would you like to tell Edward about that song?

Florence: That song, of course, is the core of my sort of recovery. That Edward wanted to thank his teachers for encouraging him to stay in school in spite of all the terrible things that had happened to him, that he has forgiven, makes him so powerful. It gives him such ability to move people's hearts. If anyone asks me today if I taught in a residential school, I can say "Yes."

After several more questions, Duncan asked us about the Truth and Reconciliation Commission (TRC).

Duncan: How do you feel about the TRC, as it travels across the country?

Edward: I think it is a much-needed process so that people can start their healing journey. So that, as people, we can walk side by side.

Duncan: I hope that both of you tell your story, because you have had your own reconciliation. You have a lesson for all of us.

The interview ended with "Survivor's Voice," the song Edward had written about his experiences at residential school.

Many listeners contacted Edward and me following the interview. Author James Bartleman, the former lieutenant-governor of Ontario, sent Edward a box of his books. Bartleman is Métis, and he has succeeded in spite of racism, as Edward did. Friends called and wrote me to say how touched they had been. A childcare worker at a residential school who had testified against an abuser wrote to the CBC, "There is nothing they didn't try to do to break me down. But I knew I was telling the truth. Now I am a stronger and better person. I feel I can stand and hold my head high and not simply be another victim."

Both Edward and I were glad we had agreed to be interviewed, though it was not an easy process. As Edward wrote to me afterwards, "Thinking about the interview, I believe we touched some people and hope they get up and start the healing process."

Chapter 17

Florence's Story: Government Apologies

In June 2008, my sister Lorna was scheduled for a serious operation. I flew to Winnipeg to be with her. Since I was there on June 11, I decided to watch the federal government's apology to Aboriginal people for the residential schools on the big screen at the Radisson Hotel. I arrived early, as I wished to attend the lunch for survivors and their families. As lunch was served, caregivers dressed in red jackets circulated to support survivors who might be triggered and upset.

At one point, I heard a voice from across the table say, "I'll go and talk to my teacher." It was Gloria York, from my first class at Norway House in 1954. How heartwarming it was to have her sit and talk with me.

Drumming and chanting began in a corner of the big room, and everyone stood as the Grand Entry, led by two proud standard bearers dressed in traditional clothing, came into the room. Following them were dancers in embroidered moccasins, fringed leather pants and beaded jackets. A stunning male dancer followed, wearing a headdress of three tall eagle feathers that spun around. A stately gentleman came next, in his veteran's uniform resplendent with medals on many-coloured ribbons. Last was a jingle dress dancer holding a three-feathered eagle fan. Behind the podium on the stage hung a purple star blanket.

When all were assembled, we were welcomed by Clarence Nepinak from the Pine Creek First Nation. An elder said a prayer, and then singers and drummers performed a song for the survivors and a victory song.

People took turns coming to the podium to speak. Chief Ron Evans, grand chief of Manitoba, who is from Norway House, hoped for healing from family violence. Another person said, "We are here. We were at the mercy of the white people—held prisoners in our own country. Let's get out of these shackles; let's be free. We are grassroots people. Load your pipes. Ask for help. Unity is the answer." Sharlene Palmer sang her version of "O Canada" in Cree.

The speeches and songs continued as everyone anxiously waited for the apology from Prime Minister Harper. Finally the big screen lit up and there was Stephen Harper, standing in the House of Commons in Ottawa surrounded by various First Nations leaders and the leaders of the three opposition parties. We listened as Harper said, "The treatment of children in Indian residential schools is a sad chapter in our history... Today we recognize that this policy of assimilation was wrong, has caused great harm and has no place in our country." When he finished, there was no applause in the ballroom.

Next, the Liberal leader, Stéphane Dion, acknowledged the role his party had played and apologized, then went around the circle of Aboriginal leaders in the Commons to shake their hands. A few people in the ballroom applauded.

NDP leader Jack Layton spoke next, saying we must begin a shared future. The residential schools had harmed heritage, language and traditions. There was sexual abuse and inadequate health care. The woman standing beside me, who had been in Stephie's class at Norway House, cried. Layton mentioned the United Nations Declaration on the Rights of Indigenous Peoples and also the need for safe drinking water. There was enthusiastic applause for him. When Gilles Duceppe of the Bloc Québécois reiterated Jack Layton's call for Canada to sign the United Nations declaration, the people in the ballroom responded with a standing ovation.

When the telecast was over, Wab Kinew, broadcaster and member of the Onigaming First Nation, asked me on camera what I'd thought of the apology. He had wanted to interview Gloria York, too, but she had to leave early.

"I agree with the apology," I said.

"Why?"

"I was sorry to find out what had happened to so many of my students."

"Why are you here?"

"Because I was there. I have reconnected with many of my former students. One more thing the government should do is to appoint a First Nations person as our next governor general."

The gathering was completed with a prayer, and the Grand Entry party led the survivors solemnly out of the Radisson Ballroom.

When I phoned Edward, my guiding light, the next day, he said, "I saw you on TV last night."

"How did I do?"

"Right on," he said.

There was no greater encouragement or more inspirational response I could have received.

Two days later, on June 13, the government of Manitoba offered its own apology to the province's nine thousand residential school survivors. The apology was to be delivered by Premier Gary Doer in the Manitoba Legislative Building.

I wanted to be there, so I took a taxi from St. Boniface Hospital, where I was visiting Lorna. I arrived early at the Legislative Building, an impressive, monumental structure fashioned of Tyndall stone quarried in Garson, Manitoba, thirty-seven kilometres northeast of Winnipeg. As a student, I'd loved walking up the long entrance boulevard to the building. Poised atop the dome, facing north, is the Golden Boy, a magnificent gilded figure and probably Manitoba's best-known symbol. He is meant to embody the spirit of enterprise and eternal youth. He carries a sheaf of golden grain in his left arm, while his right hand holds high a torch calling youth to enter the race.

The race, however, is unfair. Opportunity is unequal. The sheaf of grain irritated me, too, because by 1829 Aboriginal lands had been taken and turned into farmland. It signalled the end of life as people knew it before the arrival of the Selkirk settlers. In 1846, near present-day Selkirk, the Cree and Saulteaux (People of the Rapids) lived and practised the new agriculture very successfully. However, by 1907 the reserve had been "surrendered," and soon all the Aboriginal people were gone. In return, they'd been given swampy scrubland on the Peguis Reserve.

That day, as I walked up the broad steps and through the great front doors, I was greeted by two huge green-bronze buffaloes/bison. Of course, the great herds of these magnificent animals had been wiped out in a few short years after contact with white men, but I was still gratified to see them honoured.

I climbed the great staircase to the second floor, where many people were gathering in the rotunda. Ed Wood, an elder from St. Theresa Point and a recipient of the Order of Manitoba, gave the opening prayer, first in Cree, then Saulteaux, and then in English. MLA Eric Robinson spoke tearfully of how residential schools had torn his family apart. He had been taken from his parents when he was five and placed in a world that taught him everything he knew was wrong. His mother had been sent to residential school at the age of three, and that was the only life she knew until she turned eighteen.

Next, the White Cloud drummers were invited to sing for the survivors. As the biggest man gave one mighty beat on his drum, I felt shivers race through my body. The sound echoed through the huge, silent space. It made me think of the strap that had so often been used on Indian children. I thought of Edward with his swollen, black and blue wrists. As the three drummers played together, I wondered, would I ever really understand their suffering? No. My knowledge was like a grain of sand on an immense sweeping beach.

Then the survivors moved into the chamber. After some time, the premier and MLAs filed out to stand on the grand staircase facing east. The residential school survivors, among them distinguished, decorated veterans and chiefs, formed a second line. The two lines faced each other, then began to shake one another's hands. As the drummers climbed halfway up the steps and began a drum song, I wondered if there had ever been so many Aboriginal people in this colossal, costly edifice, so different from artistic tepees, small log cabins and caribou tents.

Chapter 18

Florence's Story: The Bell

A few days after the government apologies, I flew to Norway House to visit the Gamblins. On Sunday morning, Edward came to meet me at the York Boat Inn in his blue truck. We exchanged a long, warm hug. Then it was off to his home, where I visited with Aurelia and other family members.

The next day, I drove to Cross Lake with Edward and his friend Wayne Flett, a music promoter. They were on a jaunt to promote a concert Edward had coming up in Norway House on June 29. I was excited to accompany them. I'd only been to Cross Lake once before, in 1957, travelling by Bombardier after dark to the official opening of a new United Church there.

While Edward and Wayne set up a table in the Northern Store to sell concert tickets, I went for a walk, taking my camera. When I saw a trail leading toward a cemetery, I wandered through high grass until I found the entrance. Many of the graves had traditional white picket fences around them. Some were very old, with the paint worn off, decorated with faded wreaths. Some were new: a wonderful shiny black double-heart-shaped marker with a tiny red fire truck on top and a bigger red truck at the bottom, with pictures of young boys on the hearts. To see so many early deaths grieved me. It was shocking to me how many husbands, sons, brothers, daughters and mothers had died in their twenties, thirties and forties. I thought of Rosalie Ross, the youngest girl in the school in 1954 and a cousin of Edward's, who Ken Crassweller told me had died recently. When I arrived back at the store, I was surprised to see Edward visiting with Isabel Ross, Rosalie's sister. I offered my condolences on Rosalie's death and said I'd like to place some flowers on her grave. Isabel offered to accompany me there. Sunflowers were Rosalie's favourites, she told me. There were two engraved on her tombstone. But there were no sunflowers at the store, so I bought a swag of yellow artificial flowers. Rosalie's gravestone showed a lovely woman wearing her graduation gown and glasses. Isabel said Rosalie had become a primary teacher and had worked hard while suffering a lot of stress. She was married and had children. As we were leaving the cemetery, Isabel asked me if I remembered Carl Ross; he had also been in my class the first year. She showed me four graves together: Carl and three other men who had drowned while fishing on Cross Lake when the wind came up. Their bodies were found tangled in their nets. Carl, at twenty-five, was the youngest. Over and over, tragedies. But I told Isabel how pleased I was to meet her again.

I was thankful Edward had taken me to Cross Lake to visit his birthplace in daylight and to reconnect with my fine student Isabel. That day, he had opened another door for me.

The next morning, Wayne, Edward and I went down to the mall in Norway House, again to advertise his concert on June 29. We talked, told jokes and drank coffee.

People stopped by to talk. The first was Norman Albert, a friendly former residential school student. When I expressed my interest in going into the James Evans Memorial United Church, which was now boarded up, with the new church built beside it, Norman said he'd get permission from Reverend Olive Flett and then go down after work to take the plywood sheet off the doors.

Edward's cousin, Rosalie Ross, became a teacher at Cross Lake. She died of cancer at 41.

Edward, Aurelia and I drove down in the evening, and there was Norman with two of his friends. Olive met us there. The men had already removed the plywood. I was so grateful that Norman had arranged this for me.

We had to clamber up into the church, since the cement steps no longer existed. We walked through the old church, running our hands over the smooth varnished pews and admiring the pictures of famous people on the walls. I stopped in front of the choir loft to fondly remember the beautiful small organ that used to be up there. Long ago I had practised on it sometimes when the church was empty.

At the front, on the altar table, a Bible stood open, with vases of artificial flowers on either side. Aurelia and Edward had been married there, so I asked if I could take a picture of them standing there again. Aurelia giggled and giggled, but I captured a charming picture.

Then Norman rang the church's beautiful bell, pulling the rope again and again. The sound, so familiar to the older generation, had sent its call to worship for years across Little Playgreen Lake to Keeper's Point and Forestry Island. Memories flooded back of attending services here preached by Reverend Ken McLeod, Reverend Ibbs Avery, or one of the First Nations lay ministers. Rows and rows of quiet residential school students had filled the pews, including Edward, all of them thinking of home.

When I mentioned to Edward afterwards that Ibbs Avery had always said the Lord's Prayer in Cree, he said he remembered part of it. We drove in his truck way down to the hospital, which had barely changed since 1958, and then as far as you could go upstream to West Island, away from the reserve. Here there were fine houses with lawns and cars and boats parked in the driveways.

Driving back, Edward played me two of his newly recorded songs: "Your Name on the Cross," his lament for Virgil's suicide, and "Grandpa's Dream," a song about the old ones sensing that chaos lay ahead. Edward liked to play his songs loudly, which I liked too. This would be our last adventure together, since I was returning to Winnipeg the next day. Again, Edward and Aurelia had treated me royally since I had arrived.

When Edward and Aurelia dropped me off at the Inn, I had a hard time settling down. After a while, I put my jacket back on and walked partway to Church Point in the dark. When I turned around, I realized what had called me out. The moon, full, dressed in gold and orange, was shining on this special place, Norway House.

The weather was fine for flying the next morning. Edward, Aurelia and I had breakfast together and talked awhile. Then we were off down to the Perimeter Air terminal. Luggage checked, another picture taken of Aurelia and Edward, hugs and goodbyes. The three of us held back our emotions, for when would we see each other again?

My sister Lorna met me in Winnipeg and took me to her home for a visit. The next morning, I phoned Edward, since he'd said, "I'll expect a call from you." I told him what I'd thought of after I was on the plane—what I'd like to have said before I left. "You and Aurelia have a second home in Courtenay, and if ever either of you need me, I'll be there."

"And us for you," he replied.

On Sunday, October 12, Edward sent me the following email at 5:22 a.m.: "When writing my book it surely is painful having to go through it in detail. I usually write early in the a.m. so that tears can flow freely without holding back. Anyway, the Almighty is always here—such a comforting feeling."

Later that same day, I wrote to him about an experience I had had that morning. "I was at Christ the King Catholic Church in

Courtenay, BC, kneeling and praying beside my friend Kay Hilborn. In a flash, I was in Norway House, over your home. Every detail of the outside and then the inside appeared to me. This was the first time I had ever experienced the feeling of time travelling. I had a sensational, spiritual thrumming throughout my entire body. I found myself thinking about your words in the book that you are writing, Edward. You said, 'I waited for that *familiar* pain—it came on *like the ones before* and the *ringing that followed.*' You did not describe the trauma as '*one time Mr. S.,* etc.' I realized he must have hurt you many times."

Chapter 19 🪶

Florence's Story: Fourth Son

Could I have ever imagined in 1954 that a charming little five-year-old Cree dancer would someday become my son?

Besides my sons Glenn and Ian, I already had a third son—their longtime friend Robert, whom Glenn had known since kindergarten. One day in January 2009, as I was doing housework, a light bulb went on in my head: maybe Edward would like to become my fourth son. I emailed him about it that day.

He replied immediately, "Holding the status of 'Fourth Son' would be an honour. This little email sure is powerful. Thanks, Mom!"

In my reply, I said, "Welcome to the family, Edward. Our symbol is the ladybug, as Kaefer means ladybug, or beetle, in German. Our colours are black and red."

Later, in the mail, I sent Edward a picture of his three younger brothers, Ian, Glenn and Robert. We were all proud to add such a successful singer, writer, Native spiritual leader and speaker to our family. From then on, Edward always addressed his emails and letters to Mom or *nimama* (my mom) and signed them son or *kikosis* (your son).

It wouldn't be long before I learned the power of a traditionally adoptive mother. On February 7, Edward emailed me to say, "I've been feeling excruciating pain since yesterday; in fact it's so severe I'm in tears when the pain comes on! But I'm optimistic the procedure's gonna heal me. I am to see an ulcer specialist in Winnipeg soon.

"As a Survivor, the continuous denial by the Canadian Govt. of their abuse on native boys and girls is what hurts the most. They won't take responsibility for the injustices and murders that happened."

Chapter 20

Edward's Story: My People

Age sixteen, and leaving school, gave me the freedom to feel whatever I wanted to feel. True freedom was elusive, though. The earning of freedom came not only with age but also by having walked through the fires placed by those who thought less of me, my heritage, my culture and my people.

I remember that day I walked out from Portage Collegiate... that wind of freedom when it hit my face. The dam just broke and I stood there crying. The feeling that morning I don't think I'll ever be able to express in words, that awesome tingling in me, not knowing that I was walking into a world of dependency. I had promised myself I'd never drink but that's exactly what I did for sixteen years.

I've realized through the years why I turned to alcohol. I guess I used it to try and drown/erase/forget the pains (only for a while). Not being able to bring out the "ghosts" in me, not being able to talk about what was eating away at me on the inside, the embarrassing sexual abuse inflicted on me as a child, the shame and the filth I felt.

The morning I woke up after two months of being drunk and on skid row in Winnipeg, I managed to get up, I know, with the help of our Creator. I finally gave in fully, just being tired of hurting other people. I decided to make a change. That was thirty years ago, and with the help of Aurelia I managed. She's such a strong woman. I didn't go through AA. I guess the important thing is having someone who cares, one who'll be there whenever you need to lean on someone. I'm so thankful the Creator gave her to me to lean on, and she's so willing.

From an email: "Mom, just wanting to share. There's been an idea going around in my head—thinking of writing about the corruption etc.... I've already come up with the title: 'Black Road Walker.' It goes along with the traditional teachings about the red and black road. Later, Son."

For those who came and saw the potential of the area, Norway House sat at a very agreeable and convenient location. Those who exploited, manipulated, took and took and thought themselves superior to others around the area were just the beginning of a well-thought-out assimilation plan. This concept and their belief that they were better, due to their technological, intellectual and artistic achievements, caused painful, disrespectful relationships and clashes between the whites and First Nations. Norway House sat at a junction between two *very* different worlds.

Norway House was the gateway to the north, and due to being neatly situated and centrally placed, it was the ideal spot for a Hudson's Bay post. Because of the unique formation of the waterways, Norway House became the meeting place and storage area for freight heading inland, west or to southern trading posts. Those who hunted and raised their families on whatever they could obtain from Mother Earth were able to trade and sell the much-sought-after furs they trapped. Many locals were employed by the trade king, the Hudson's Bay Company.

History tells us by word of mouth about the cultural and traditional way of life of the Cree/Ininiw who lived in the area.

The Cree were nomadic, following the movement of the animals they needed for survival. It was a harsh environment, and those who chose to raise a family in the area found it very unforgiving and difficult. Norway House was mainly swampland, and the only outcropping of rock and somewhat prime land was found along Keeci-Sipi, the mighty Nelson River.

When the Hudson's Bay Company first came in to establish a post in 1814, they had with them "men of the cloth," the Black Robes. They were from different denominations: Catholics, Anglicans and Methodists. The pushing of their beliefs onto the local people, with the assumption that one would not see everlasting life unless one practised Christian ideals, destroyed the Cree people's feeling of pride in who they were and demeaned their way of life. The eliminating of the people's cultural and traditional belief system is still evident today, only now it's being done by the First Nations themselves against those people who choose to practise traditional forms of worship.

The first Methodist boarding school was built in Norway House about 1893 and later burned down. A second one was built in 1914. The third one opened in 1954. There was also a Catholic Indian Residential School in Norway House. These schools were jointly run by the federal government and the churches. By those who ran them, these schools were seen as necessary if the government's assimilation plan was to succeed. Back in 1920, a bill had been passed in Parliament to rid the country of its "Indian problem." So started the plan, that shameful and darkest period in Canadian history, a painful fire many unfortunate First Nations girls and boys had to walk through, not by their choosing. The sacred bond, the fine thread that love had spun together was severed by the genocidal process masterminded by the Canadian government.

One question cuts a clean, painful path to the soul: Most Sacred Spirit, why is it Canada still does not want to know?

The government henchmen, that appointed body of supposedly caring and loving individuals belonging to the dominant religious entities to which the Canadian government had transferred its obligations, were supposed to provide quality education, care and direction to the children. It's amazing, considering the historical interaction between the foreign people who arrived and the landlords of Turtle Island, how these pushy, arrogant and heartless people came to stand on unconquered soil. They were a people who had somehow convinced themselves and their offspring that they were the chosen race, having *all* say as to what should be included in treaties that they have yet to live up to. It is hard to fathom how a people guided by biblical principles and values can mistreat, lie, cheat and be so greedy as to steal land and resources from the trusting, unsuspecting keepers of Kakanadak Uski (Sacred Land).

In the years following first contact, the rights and freedoms of the indigenous people were easily swept under filthy rugs. The foreigners who had appointed themselves to be in charge managed to segregate our people onto lands that had no value and which our people would never be able to make use of economically. Once they had achieved this, they were then free to make laws without our inclusion and participation. This dominant society masterminded the abusive system they labelled the Indian residential schools, where First Nations children suffered unfathomable atrocities at the hands of perverts and overzealous religious fanatics.

Because of these unfortunate misdealings and the labelling of another race of people as savage and stupid, First Nations children suffered undue abuses at the hands of those who thought they had a better system.

Now, having had the experience as an adult of sitting across the negotiating table from representatives of the federal government and the Churches, having had to listen to their denials and their excuse that "it was the system back then," I remain dumbfounded. No wonder it is hard for the general public to take responsibility for this dark and shameful past and the crimes committed against our people.

As an Aboriginal, I question how anyone can be proud of such a shameful history. If my ancestors had passed a history like this onto me, I would have tears full of shame and embarrassment rolling down my cheeks.

In December 2001, I sent the following letter to the United Nations high commissioner for human rights on behalf of my people:

December 19, 2001

The High Commissioner for Human Rights of the United Nations
Palais des Nations
1211 Geneva 10, Switzerland

Re: Demand for Immediate Action

To whom it may concern,

For informational purposes I was an inmate of the Norway House Indian Residential School, Norway House, Manitoba, Canada, from 1954 to 1965. This facility was run by the United Church of Canada and funded by the Federal Government of Canada. I was only five years old when they sentenced me to the institution mentioned. At such an early age, how was I to know the purpose for my removal from a loving environment and locked up in a scary and frightful place? In the institution mentioned I experienced sexual and physical abuse, loss of identity/cultural shaming and damage, loss of family/community bonding, unlawful confinement, to name but a few. While those that suffered atrocities/other damages in the residential schools are at an age when the only comforting thought is an early grave, those that had inflicted the "PAIN" are pointing fingers and not wanting to take responsibility or hiding behind laws they had masterminded like the Statute of Limitation Act of Manitoba, Canada. They continue to come up with other stall tactics while the elderly are dying off.

I am, at this time, begging and demanding that, because of their role in administering the Indian residential schools and conducting atrocities and murders at related facilities, and covering up these crimes, the government of Canada, the RCMP and the Catholic, United and Anglican Churches be charged with complicity in Genocide before the International Criminal Court, and other appropriate United Nations bodies.

Please inform me personally when you have received this. Please inform me by letter. Thank you, and I remain...

In the Spirit of Healing,

Edward Gamblin
Norway House, Manitoba, Canada

I also wrote poetry as a form of therapy and an outlet for anger. The poems are geared toward the Church and the government. I guess my writing could be looked at as a form of healing.

Untitled

In front of me a book
For years left unopened
The child within wants out
The child within wants, needs.
What's the want? What's the need?
Did not feel, did not receive
How could he know? To know is to open!
Relive the hurt, relive the pain
Relive the nightmare…What a dreaded journey!

Five years old, another night I do not want
Vile, demented groping hand
Tears, tears—can't you see the tears?
Oh, Most Holy Spirit, feel my hurts, feel my pain
The child not knowing it would be a lonely eleven years.

Through hazy reality I hear my woman moan
My precious baby girl crying
No milk—both breasts too sore to feed
Why? Why?…I need to heal.

Do not deny me again, O Canada and Most Holy Book
A feather held high
I stand exposed like an open book.
This is not my shame! I did not consent!
I do not want your shame, O Canada!

God grant me the serenity
I'm a victim, I'm a product
Wounded but still a warrior
A survivor
This cycle will break!

Official Approval

Officially sanctioned by CHURCH and STATE;
Like the Wannsee Protocol, 1 a murderous system and ideology
Gave reason to why Grandpa could not love
He did time in a mainstream denomination, legal institution
And was forced to be part of a well-intentioned experiment
Dr. Mengele would be so proud of Canada's radial hygienists
And let's not forget Adolph Hitler!

The CHURCH's angel of death, A.E. Caldwell
Said my people lacked civilized thought and spirit
I guess this is why he thought it was okay to kill
That it was alright "to kill the Indian within the Indian"
With, of course, the blessings of the CHURCH and STATE
They stripped my Grandpa of his legal and civil rights
Which I think would make their genocidal acts a National Crime.

Who gave this official howl of approval,
Knowing that there were wolves within the fold?
This is the highest evil, in the guise of religious moralism
Rome, you authorized this systematic brutality and murder
This is termed Crimes Against Humanity by the Convention
Have you or your Black Robes any conscience at all?
Do you remember the names of those 50,000 you buried?

They have yet to look TRUTH in the face
Destroying a People was their official policy
What is the word: assimilation? or annihilation?
There are thousands waiting and waiting and waiting...
While you are busy pointing at each other
Ask me who the guilty party is
Better yet...ask those 50,000 in unmarked graves.

Ever remembered...the 50,000 Native children, the nameless faces
who met their untimely fate in a Canadian Institution, somewhere...

Chapter 21 🪶

Florence's Story: Edward's Heroes

It is said that in North America before the white people arrived with horses and guns in the early 1800s, there were approximately seventy million buffalo that the First Nations revered and honoured. Aboriginal people began to kill more buffalo when they too had horses and guns, so that they could barter for the white man's goods. Soon government policy became such that if all the buffalo were killed, the settlers could easily starve the First Nations out and have their land, and 7.5 million buffalo were killed in two years. By 1880 the slaughter was over. Only a few hundred buffalo remained, protected in Yellowstone National Park in the US, and the Aboriginal populations were destitute.

In the late fifteenth century, there are thought to have been two million Aboriginal people in Canada. By the end of the nineteenth century, only 100,000 were left—a depopulation of 95 percent. Shocking. Aboriginal people were treated no better than the buffalo.

The almost endless plains were once the homeland of the great Cree Chief Big Bear, or Mistahimaskwa, born in 1825. As John Ralston Saul wrote in *A Fair Country*,[1] "There were great leaders such as Big Bear and Poundmaker who manoeuvred, delayed, argued and put forth alternate approaches to how the vast plains should be organized as the settlers poured in." Soon,

"Some of the greatest leaders Canada had produced, Big Bear and Poundmaker, were in prison and broken."

In his music Edward sings about his heroes. He sings of "Poundmaker ridin' in the rain" and "the day Big Bear's dreams came to an end" on "that cold Manitubah[2] Mountain." Edward told me that he was never taught in school about his own peoples' heroes, such as Poundmaker, Big Bear and Louis Riel, only about English or American ones. But he read voraciously, and he learned on his own about his many heroes.

"That cold Manitubah Mountain" that Edward writes about is Stony Mountain Penitentiary, north of Winnipeg, where Big Bear was jailed for two years because he refused to accept a small reserve north of the good farmland, where his people would be fed bacon and flour. Big Bear argued against this, demanding a large piece of land where his people could continue to live as they always had.

The presiding judge, Judge Richardson, said, "I have no objection to hear what you have to say, but on one point you must be corrected. The land never belonged to you. The land was and is the Queen's. She has allowed you to use it."

Edward told me about Big Bear's powers. "Big Bear would leave the prison and go out and dance on the grass. The junior guards were worried about this, as they would be blamed, so they just said nothing. After a while Big Bear would be back in his cell."

Big Bear was released from jail early because he was old and sick. His son took him to the Little Pine Reserve, in Saskatchewan, so he could see his beloved prairies again. Big Bear died on January 17, 1888, age sixty-three, and was buried at Poundmaker Reserve, Cut Knife, Saskatchewan.

At the time of his own death, Edward was sixty-two, a year younger than his hero.

Chapter 22

Florence's Story: Warriors

In a series of emails, Edward began to express more and more concerns about his health and Aurelia's. He seemed to be almost constantly on the road. "Aurelia's the same; we're still waiting for the people from the Public Health to take action. Geez...they sure don't realize how important it is for them to start the process. At times it's so hard to keep the optimism happening, especially for Aurelia, as she gets so agitated when we can't understand what she's trying to convey. They're having the Annual York Boat Days here this week, but I have to leave for Beauval, SK, as I was invited to their Gospel Jamboree as a guest speaker. My presentation is actually about my personal experiences in the residential school. But I'm focusing mainly on the healing process—how I was eventually able to bring out those demons and start on my healing journey. Anyway, I'm taking my new Gospel album with me, and I surely hope it sells."

A few weeks later he wrote:

I just returned from Thompson, where I did a week-long gig. That sure takes a great deal out of me. I arrived back with a swollen knee, but that goes after a few days' rest. While there, I was invited to speak again on residential experiences. It's just as hard as when I first started opening up. I guess it'll never go away.

As the weeks and months passed, Edward's emails began to show signs of his growing frustrations.

I just received another invitation out to The Pas; same subject, but to include my healing journey. Aurelia's been somewhat under the weather. Still no movement to get her into speech therapy. I'm starting to wonder why. Maybe it's too costly for Indian Affairs? The community's been experiencing shortages of doctors and extended health care. We have two resident doctors to look after a community of eight to ten thousand. Speaking of 'breach of treaties'! Most look forward to their last breath, especially the elderly...what a pity! At least then, they say, the suffering stops. Oops! Sorry for sounding angry.

Thanks for your friendship.

The struggle to perform and keep earning money for his family, in spite of his leg problems and his worries about Aurelia's health, must have been very draining and disheartening for Edward. He was becoming so successful with his music and his public speaking; he deserved to relax and enjoy life instead.

On March 10, 2009, Edward wrote, "Nimama—my mom: I just couldn't stand the pain anymore. I was up puking half the night and all morning so badly I checked myself in for an amputation. I fly out today at 4:45. I'll be in St. Boniface by the time you receive this email."

Rick, Edward's producer, was the last person to talk to Edward in the hospital before he went down the hall for major surgery. His leg was amputated above the knee.

After that, Rick visited Edward every day, and I called him to get regular reports. I called Lorna, and she said she'd drive down to visit Edward in hospital. As I walked with friends by the ocean in Courtenay, I tried to send my thoughts to Edward, to give him the strength to keep believing he would get better.

Lorna called to say she'd seen Edward. His family was there, including his son Jared. They'd driven nine hours to get there. Edward was feeling chipper, Lorna said, sitting up in bed wearing a fine leather cap with one of his nicknames, "Latchie," written on it. He told Lorna he expected to be home in about a week.

An email from Edward arrived on April 1.

Hi Mom! Well, I'm back home now and waiting for the incision to heal and the swelling to go down. Approximately a month from now, I'll be returning to Winnipeg for further physio and to be fitted with an artificial leg. The main thing is...the nagging intolerable pain is now gone!

They medevaced Candida, my oldest daughter, out to Winnipeg last week and she was in intensive care at the Grace Hospital. I was able to visit her before I came home and she was doing ok. Then yesterday the nurse said they were moving her to the upstairs part of the Hosp. which means she is really healing. She had been medevaced due to hypothermia and she was low in potassium.

Wow! This has been a real trying year for us, but the trust and belief in the Higher Power is still there. Later.

Your son,
Edward
...Aurelia is doing ok!

On April 17, Edward wrote:

Aurelia can't seem to gain weight even though she's eating OK. I'm kinda worried about her and my daughter. Candida is forever having stomach pains. It seems like my pain too is returning. It's that phantom pain... the brain has not accepted there is a limb missing. It's not as bad as before though.
May the angels protect you til next we chat!

Your son,
Edward

A few days later, another email from Edward arrived.

The idiot and murderer, Columbus, is the guy who started the ball rolling about who he thought we were. It amazes me how people can celebrate the idiot's stupidity! Columbus Day...Geez!...And yet it's with us today. It's a good thing he wasn't looking for Turkey... we'd be called Turkeys!

Anyway, howz Mom these days? Howz your health? Aurelia's going for her appointment this Thursday and my youngest sister Cindy's escorting her out to Winnipeg. She'll be OK. She just can't seem to gain weight even though she's eating. I hope they find out what's the matter with her.

The phantom pain's sickening and it's keeping me up nights. I wonder when it's all gonna end?

Well, til next time, may the Creator be with you, Mom!
Your son,
Edward

I phoned Edward when I discovered he was in the hospital for therapy to become accustomed to his artificial leg. He was always in pain afterwards, he said, but he had graduated from parallel bars to a walker. He had to learn to fall and get up again, and so on. What a journey!

Chapter 23

Florence's Story: Holding My Feather

In May 2009 Richard Wright wrote an article about Edward and me that was published in the *United Church Observer*.[1] The title of the article was "I Remember You. You Were My Teacher," and the story's cutline read, "As National Truth and Reconciliation efforts stall, a former student and his teacher start a remarkable journey of mutual healing."

In his interview with Richard Wright, Edward made it clear how the sexual abuse had affected him. "All the pain left an indelible mark on Gamblin," Wright wrote. "He was emotionally frozen, incapable of developing male friendships. Intimacy with women was a problem, too. Though married, he cheated on his wife repeatedly in an attempt to prove to himself and to the community that sexual abuse by a man hadn't stunted his heterosexual machismo...Gamblin has overcome his philandering impulse and is proud of his 39 years of marriage." Edward was celebrating thirty years of sobriety, too, Wright wrote.

Wright closed his article by quoting Edward's thoughts on reconciliation. "The final truth he's learned about reconciliation is that it will not be one grand, finite act. It will be a multitude of small acts and gestures played out between individuals, and it will be ongoing until all the wounds are healed. Says Gamblin, 'It doesn't seem to work any other way.'"

For Edward's sixty-first birthday on May 17, I sent him a water-colour painting of Poundmaker, a handsome leader of the Cree who rode with Big Bear. It arrived on time, and he was very excited. He wrote:

> Thanks a million. What a surprise! Chief Poundmaker earned his name because he was a remarkable leader who could build the best "pounds," or corrals, to capture buffalo. A reserve in Saskatchewan is named after him. His Cree name was Pihtokahanaiwirjin. I was like a kid opening his X-mas present on X-mas morning. Although we never had presents while at school, I guess I picked up on how to be excited from my grandkids when they open their gifts.
>
> Luv ya and thx again.

I had been attending Christ the King Catholic Church in Courtenay with a friend, and I'd been asked to give a talk about residential schools on Aboriginal Day, June 21, at Comox United Church. When I told Edward I was making this presentation, I asked him for some guidance regarding his song "Survivor's Voice," which I planned to feature.

> Hi Mom,
> For your presentation, I'll be saying prayers and asking the Creator and the Grandfathers to be with you for support. This should be as good as any time to further explain as to the contents of the song.
>> Her words cut like a knife. "How come you never say you love me, Daddy?"
>> Explanation: These lines stress the fact that we

had no role models to copy; the bond between the child and the parents/community was severed.

Verse one is self-explanatory: "They" is geared toward not only the Church but the federal government as well. They never took into account that maybe we had been taught by our parents/community *our* way of worshipping and acknowledging the Creator and His Helpers. The abuser was not only the individual who got his/her jollies in fondling/molesting young innocent children. The federal government and the Church were just as guilty of this heinous crime!

The second verse tells about the overly strict rules and regulations, not having to bother about planning your day's activities as they were done for you, and the patterning of the brain, making you into something you could never be, the daily derogatory remarks about your origin, and the physical/sexual abuse. There was also deliberate omission of the Aboriginal assistance into the making of Canada and our achievements. We had no heroes. In fact, we used to cheer for the cowboy when we were watching movies.

The chorus tells of when I was at the negotiating table with the federal government and the Church. When we stood up to tell our experiences, they had a hard time keeping eye contact. The representatives from both the government and the Church were always telling the survivor to heal. You would think the one who really needed healing was the abuser! Their excuse was always, "It was the government and Church at the time." It seemed they found it hard to listen with their hearts.

The third verse tells of how by constantly calling down our people, our elders, our form of worship, they led me to eventually feeling ashamed of my own people. As well, it tells of the severing of the family bond between child and his or her parents and community.

I'm hoping this will help in your presentation. And I'm hoping the message of "healing together" will open some hearts!

—In the Spirit of Healing, your son, Edward.

On the day of my talk, I arrived early at Comox United Church to make arrangements with the sound man to play Edward's song "Survivor's Voice," starting it at the exact spot where I wanted it.

As the day opened, Reverend Maggie Enwright led the special service in prayer: "May we find peace with First Nations people who are reeling with change disproportionate to other Canadians." She had arranged for the service to have an Aboriginal focus in every aspect: prayers, suitable hymns and a ceremony that had the congregation face the four sacred directions and the centre, with appropriate prayers for each direction.

I wore gifts given to me by two residential school students I taught in 1954. From Emily Workman (Ellis), I had a blue and white beaded necklace and earrings. From Caroline Cheekie (Yassie), red and white beaded moccasins trimmed with white rabbit fur. They were both Sayisi Dené women from Churchill. And from Stephie, with whom I had first gone to Norway House, I had received an eagle pin. I thought of the verse from the Bible, Isaiah 40:31: "But they that wait upon the Lord shall renew their strength; they shall mount up with wings as eagles."

When it was my turn to speak, I gathered up my papers and my feather. Because I was wearing moccasins, I did not make a sound as I left the pew and walked the few steps to the lectern. It was the second time I had carried my feather to give a talk.

"We were both beginners in 1954," I began, "Edward five years old in kindergarten and I in my first year teaching, at age nineteen. I had been brought up by a mother who believed all people were equal, and I jumped at the chance to teach Indian children. They were wonderful, bright, talented students. I did not try to change them in any way.

"I was not aware of the abuse that went on in the dormitories or the playrooms at the school," I told the congregation. "When I found this out after reconnecting with Edward, I was dismayed, and I could never think of teaching in Norway House ever again in the same way."

When I played "Survivor's Voice," the song filled every corner in the large sanctuary.

"Edward is still looking for the elusive 'We're sorry,'" I said. "I hope my talk and his song will open some hearts and that healing will happen." I closed with the words, "A residential school teacher and her student."

People clapped when I'd finished speaking. Many people came and talked to me afterwards.

Later that day, I went down to the Aboriginal celebrations in Courtenay. I walked around enjoying the beadwork, carvings and knitted sweaters. In the evening, I watched the telecast of Aboriginal Day from Whitehorse. A group of Sayisi Dené men drumming was a highlight. I thought of the Dené boys from Churchill I had taught—Peter, Alex, Sandy, Joe and Jimmy.

Chapter 24

Florence's Story: Survivors

Aurelia had been sick and losing weight for some time. In November, Edward emailed me.

> Aurelia just can't get better. She's now just skin and bones, that's how much weight she's lost. She's just gradually wasting away in front of us. It's so frustrating how the medical field can be so heartless. I don't know what kind of doctor we have. Elsewhere she'd be admitted and given proper, quality care. It's so painful having to watch this. She needs a referral from the doctor here for action to be taken. I'm wondering: any chance you can talk to him? Tell him I've been talking to you about my concern regarding her chronic weight loss, and if he can get an IV happening. She needs to gain weight prior to having anything done anyway, as she doesn't have the strength to endure any kind of medical procedure. I'm worried.

Glad to help in any way I could, I phoned the number Edward gave me for the doctor. I explained why I had phoned him: I was concerned about Aurelia Gamblin.

He replied, "Oh, yes, I know Aurelia very well."

I asked, "Could you please see her in the hospital? Her husband is very worried about her."

"Who are you? Are you a doctor?" he asked.

"No, but I taught at the United Church Indian Residential School in the 1950s." That seemed to change his attitude.

"Tell Mr. Gamblin to bring his wife in."

I was astounded but relieved. I wondered, why did my request for attention have more weight than Edward's? Was it just another example proving that racism and colonialism are alive and well in Canada?

Aurelia was diagnosed with double pneumonia and flown to Thompson, Manitoba, where there is a big mine, and therefore a somewhat better hospital. She remained there until early January.

Edward emailed me then to say that Aurelia was home, but still on oxygen and not doing well. He mentioned that he was headed to Winnipeg for a medical appointment himself, since his leg was still bothering him.

"I'm so glad our paths crossed," he wrote. "The Creator with his infinite wisdom knew I needed you in my life. You always settle the chaos in me whenever we connect. Thank you so much. In closing, 1:30…the pain is keeping me up. Well, Mom, we pray our Creator will send His love for comfort, and we love you!"

Edward went back and forth to Winnipeg for treatment for his amputated leg. A new doctor at the Health Science Centre told him he had never needed his leg amputated; the trouble had started with his liver. Edward told me he believed his liver problem stemmed from the leaking sewer lagoon that had been built, against regulations, too close to his and others' property. In the spring, the creek that ran from the lagoon and out under a bridge near his house turned brown.

On February 7 I talked to Edward, who was back home. The doctors had made an incision in his good leg and put in another artery from somewhere else. On February 13 my sister Lorna phoned to say she had been to Winnipeg and visited Edward. Lorna informed me he seemed quite chipper and would go home on Tuesday—no pain now.

Edward was so pleased that he would be back home soon, cured and healthy again.

Chapter 25 🪶

Florence's Story: Visiting Aurelia

By early April, Aurelia was receiving oxygen around the clock. She was still at home, in a hospital bed in the living room, with her family around her for 24/7 care. I had a portentous feeling I might never see her again if I didn't go now. Edward told me tears came to Aurelia's eyes when she heard I was on my way to visit her.

So I flew again over the Georgia Strait, the Coast Mountains and the Rockies and was finally once again in the prairies, my birthplace. These were the homelands of the Blackfoot, Piegan, Cree and Plains people, the domain of Red Crow, Poundmaker and Big Bear. This once sweeping landscape was now divided into sections indicated by straight lines as far as the eye could see.

Edward's tall, handsome son Jared met me outside the terminal and took my suitcase. I followed him into the waiting room, and there, sitting quietly in his wheelchair in his trademark black leather jacket and cap, was Edward. I bent to give him a heartfelt hug.

Jared carried my suitcase out to his dad's truck and then helped his dad into the driver's seat, putting his wheelchair and crutches in the back. Edward drove us down the familiar road past birch and fir trees, houses, schools and churches. As usual, I checked into the York Boat Inn.

Later that afternoon, Edward called for me with his brother Mike. We went for a drive around the community, where familiar views brought back memories. We ended up at Northend Cemetery, once located in wilderness, and now right beside a place where the road crew blasts rock. "No peace even in death," Edward said. "I want to be buried on the very edge of this cemetery, not in the middle—a simple grave for a simple man."

"Do you have that in writing?" I asked.

"No, but Mike will look after it."

That evening, with an aching heart, I made a visit to my adopted daughter, Aurelia. She was lying hooked up to the oxygen machine, incredibly thin and pale, unable to turn on her own. Her lovely, long black hair was scattered across her pillow. I sat beside her and held her small, lifeless hand. I bent and kissed her and said, "I love you." She rubbed my arm, offering me her charming smile. I gave her a small, red and white heart-shaped wall hanging. She indicated where she wanted it hung.

As I sat with Edward's family in this quiet, loving home, I felt angry that Aurelia was receiving only minimal care. She should have been in Winnipeg, where the best doctors could make a valiant effort to save her life. She was only sixty-two. Her Cree name was Asini-Iskwew, meaning Stone Woman.

I asked Edward if I could stay for a few hours. Jared brought out a mattress, and I bedded down beside Aurelia. Jane, their youngest daughter, stayed up sitting beside her mother.

My phone at the motel rang at 4 a.m. It was Edward, telling me they were taking Aurelia by ambulance to the hospital. "I'll pick you up," he said. Aurelia had not responded to her pills, he told me, so the family had decided to call the ambulance.

We arrived at the hospital before the ambulance. The medics

had tried to start an IV but could not find her small, fragile veins. So two nurses in emergency worked for some time and finally found one. It hurt Aurelia so much, but Jane was there to comfort her. She remained distressed, so Jane asked if she wanted her husband. Edward came in his wheelchair, held her hand and gave her a big, loving, warm smile that lit his face from one side to the other. Aurelia's vital signs were good. A practitioner checked her and said she was dehydrated, but her lungs were clear, so she could have the entire bag of fluid and then go home.

Then the doctor asked about home care. Edward said there was just the family. No one else was coming—the home care ordered was not showing up. I hoped the doctor would check on the order and arrange to get some extra help coming again.

When we arrived back at the house, I helped Candida make supper. I made the salad, washed dishes and set the table. Candida fried pickerel fillets and boiled some potatoes. It was a delicious supper. They seldom ate dessert, which was smart. No one was overweight or had diabetes.

Over the next few days, I visited whenever I could. Sometimes Edward sat quietly over by the stereo, playing songs for Aurelia on his guitar and mouth organ. I was touched to see their love for one another, after all they had been through.

He sang part of "Shelter From the Storm," from his CD *Bright Blue Moon:*

> She's bin that rock that you lean on
> She's bin your shelter from the rain
> The light that leads you through the storm
> You build your dreams on that stone.

When Aurelia felt well enough, she smiled at me and pressed my hand.

One afternoon Edward and I sat out on his deck for a while, enjoying a beautiful, peaceful April day, his dog Fifty lying beside us. Edward noticed birds flying high above us, at first just specks. As they began to circle slowly downward, we could see they were eagles, effortlessly soaring. We watched them for a long time, until eventually they drifted to the east. I believed the Creator had sent them just for the Gamblins and me. I'd never seen eagles in Norway House before.

I passed a bit of time walking up the hill behind the trailer where I could see the lake. Fifty loved to come along, jumping up on me and wanting me to throw him a stick. He was a big dog, with long golden hair and amber eyes.

One evening Edward harmonized softly with his harmonicas while listening to CDs by Kimmie Rhodes, Waylon Jennings and Willie Nelson. I sat next to him and kept time to the music. Aurelia seemed to find the music comforting. Edward went over and talked to her, gently teased her and made her laugh.

The next day Edward and I visited the principal of the Helen Betty Osborne School. I had brought along a book one of my grade 6 classes had made, called "Cree Moons." The students had illustrated the twelve full moons: for example, the Moon of Berries. The principal was Edward's cousin, and we had a nice visit. She told me one of the grade 3 classes was doing a similar project.

That evening, Edward's daughter phoned my hotel room to say her dad had a fever and had gone to the hospital. When I phoned later to ask how he was, his daughter told me, "The doctor just laughed at him. My dad said he was worried about septicemia, because he has had so many bypasses. But the doctor laughed again and sent him home. His fever is down now."

Stella Bailey, one of my 1954 students, had lost her son Bradford in a house fire. Edward and I had planned to go to the memorial together, but with Edward not feeling well, I went

Music was cathartic for Edward. It fed his spirit.

alone. Stella treated me as a guest of honour, seating me beside her. At the close of the memorial, we all went out to a bonfire, and each of us was given a lighted candle. More prayers were said, and the wind blew my candle out. I struggled to join in on the Lord's Prayer. I'd always found saying the prayer hard after learning of Edward's abuse at the school.

The days flew by. Edward looked tired the next time I saw him. He'd been to the hospital for blood tests, and apparently he was low on potassium and protein and was dehydrated. Christopher Ross's wife brought him a big pot of Canada goose soup.

René Paupanekis had invited me for supper, and she served a lovely meal. She lived alone, since her husband had died of cancer. Her house was filled with beautiful things.

When René drove me back to Edward's, his truck was not there. It turned out his fever was back, and he'd gone to Emergency. I was sick with worry about him. I knew he was planning a gathering and a pipe ceremony with Albert Ross for the next night, and he'd also arranged for us to go to Cross Lake to speak together. Was this too much for him? I worried that my visit was causing him too much stress.

Edward returned home, but he went to Emergency again the next evening. This time, Jared and I went with him. His two sisters, Joyce and Lorna, both nurses, were there with the doctor. Again Edward complained of his fever and a terrible pain in his back. All the doctor said was, "You know you have to eat three meals a day and drink lots of water." He didn't even examine Edward to find exactly where the pain was. Thinking back, I wish I had spoken up. The hospital kept Edward overnight, but he told me later that the doctor had spoken to him with more respect when I was there.

I was scheduled to leave Norway House the next day. Edward's daughter took me first to see Aurelia. I held her hands and looked into her dark eyes. She smiled as always. I told her I hoped she'd be feeling better soon, and that my heart stayed with her. As I left I wondered if I'd ever see her again.

Next, two of Edward's daughters and their children took me down to see Edward in the hospital. He was sitting up in bed with his cap on. He needed to have more blood tests, he said, and maybe some antibiotics. His leg had been so sore during the night that he'd been screaming, he told us, but no one came. He said the doctor would probably send him to Winnipeg. I'd be visiting Lorna for a few days, I told him, so I'd see him there. That made it easier to leave. Angelique drove me to my plane.

It was a bumpy landing in Winnipeg. Lorna, her daughter Cathy and her husband, Doug, were there to meet me. We went to a fine restaurant for a bountiful lunch. It was culture shock for me. The discrepancy between the reserve and wealthy Winnipeg!

Left to right: Nadine WIlliams, Edward's grandson Stevie Ray, Angelique, Candida, Jared, Florence's sister Lorna and Edward's dog Fifty.

What must it be like for First Nations young adults to come here to continue their education or find work, I thought.

When I phoned Edward's home that evening, his daughter Jane answered. "They airlifted Dad to Thompson," she told me. "He had a blood infection. I'll tell him you called."

After we hung up, I prayed for the Creator to protect my First Nations family tonight.

Chapter 26 🖋

Florence's Story: Look Up and See the Eagles

The next day I learned that Edward was in Winnipeg at the Health Sciences Centre. He had a blood infection from his stents: septicemia. It was just as he had feared the night the doctor at Norway House had told him to eat three meals a day and drink lots of water. Septicemia is very hard on the kidneys, thus the severe pain in his back. My heart ached. Only his family could see him, but he was my adopted son, so I was allowed in.

I had to gown and glove up before I could visit Edward in intensive care. When I saw him through the glass, it took my breath away. As I entered, Edward lay deathly still, his eyes firmly shut, his body splayed at an angle, a tube down his throat, dried blood around his mouth. There were IVs plunged into his swollen arms. The room was filled with blinking monitors of every description.

I gently stroked his hair and started to talk to him. When I asked the nurse if he'd be able to hear me, she replied, "Oh, yes. He is only sedated so he won't struggle."

Tears running down my face, I implored him to stay on this side. "Your family's waiting for you at home," I said softly. "May the Creator walk with you and all the Grandmothers and Grandfathers protect you." I thanked him for his stories, his friendship and his music. "I love you with all my heart." I cried and cried. It was hard to leave. I had to exit his room by the side door, leave my gloves and gown in a barrel and wash my hands. The nurse gave me Kleenex and asked me, "Are you all right?" I looked into her eyes, unable to answer, and left. I could not speak to Lorna. I couldn't speak in the elevator of the parkade or when we drove off toward the airport. I sat in the back of the car and looked over at the hospital.

Finally, I could say a few words. "He's on a breathing machine." They dropped me off at the airport—no place to park, so I took up my bags. Lorna said, "I'm sorry you're having such a hard time," and then they were gone as my plane was leaving soon.

As my plane took off, I looked down at Winnipeg. The things I saw were the city's two rivers, the Red and the Assiniboine, and the Golden Boy facing north on the legislative buildings. The north, I thought, where health care for First Nations people is so inadequate.

Back home that evening, I sat in my living room listening to Edward's CDs. At one point, I stepped out onto my deck to admire my big Garry oak silhouetted against the night sky, the moon, the stars and the vast universe. I thought of Edward out there visiting Big Bear, his son Virgil and his mother, who all directed him, "Not yet. Go back."

Over the weeks that followed, I stayed in close touch with Edward's family by phone. The doctor had tried to take Edward off dialysis, but then had to put him back on. However, his heart was growing stronger and was now beating on its own. The doctors determined that his blood pressure was good so he could finally come off full dialysis, and would only need it every second day. Edward couldn't talk yet, but he understood everything. I sent along my love.

Slowly Edward began to recover, and they moved him out of intensive care. The doctors wanted to perform a tracheotomy, so that he could breathe more easily. Edward was fearful it would affect his singing voice. But the head doctor assured him a tracheotomy would actually be better for his vocal cords.

Edward's blood pressure dropped. He was given more fluids to bring it up again. In the end, his doctor was able to take the respirator out without a tracheotomy. Great news.

But it was not to last. Edward's condition soon deteriorated again. He told one of his daughters, "Get Cassie to get my wheelchair in here. I'm going home," but he rambled on and kept repeating things. I was terrified he'd suffered brain damage, but his daughter suspected it was the powerful sleeping pills the doctors were giving him. "He's a residential school survivor," she said. "He never sleeps more than two hours." By now, the whole Gamblin family was in crisis. Aurelia was back in the hospital, and one daughter was also sick. The nurses had Edward sitting up. His catheter was out and he was eating protein, but he was still on dialysis. I sent him a card, including Stephie's eagle pin.

I kept up my prayers, calling on all the Grandmothers and Grandfathers. I was worried because I had not heard from Jane, and I felt scared and lonely, crying at home by myself. I phoned Jane twice—no answer. I hoped it was not bad news, but that she was at the hospital all day. Weather permitting, I went out each evening to study the night sky, Venus magnificent in the west. As I prayed, I realized that Edward was my teacher.

I'd been invited to visit my brother-in-law Rainer and his family in Hamburg, and my departure date soon arrived. After two full weeks of travel, I got home on May 31. I woke at 2 a.m., having dreamed I was in a circular space that felt like an inner sanctum, flat on my back and absolutely alone. Perhaps I had been in one too many medieval cathedrals in Germany.

Discombobulated, I got up to check my email.

In the morning, I checked in with Edward's family, then called him on his cell phone. He answered and was pleased to hear from me. When I asked how he was, he said he had an infected bedsore and a sore back, a disc problem. When he rang his bell it took too long for a nurse to come, he said, and he'd asked the Norway House chief to advocate on his behalf. Things had improved after that. It was wonderful to hear Edward laugh again. Some of my fear and pain slipped away.

But Aurelia was in hospital again for observation, and when I arrived home from my grandson Owen's birthday party on June 4, there was a message on my machine from Edward. "Bad news," he said, and then something indistinguishable. When the phone rang, it was Edward's daughter Jane. Aurelia had died that day.

When I reached Edward, he could barely speak. "I'm coming to see you," I said. "I'll see you Saturday morning." He replied, "I'll be waiting for you. Later."

So quiet, so hurt, so overwhelmed.

Chapter 27 🪶

Florence's Story: A Dream Catcher

Before I left for Winnipeg, I looked for something I could take to Edward. Aurelia had given me a soft beige dream catcher one time when I visited Norway House, and that caught my eye. I wrapped it carefully and tucked it into my bag.

Before entering Edward's hospital room, visitors had to gown and glove up. When I walked in to see him that sad morning, I returned the dream catcher to Edward.

"Do you remember this?" I asked.

He was very touched. "Yes, I remember it," he said. "Hang it right over there with the sweetgrass, where I'll see it and think of you. I'll remember your genuineness and caring."

We held hands and shed tears together.

"Why are all these terrible things happening?" Edward asked me. "Around every corner there is trouble. Why? But it hasn't shaken my faith."

After we'd talked for a while, he told me, "I knew it was coming. When I said goodbye to Aurelia before I left for Thompson, her hand reached out, grasping for something. I've heard when people do this they are picking the fruit from the Tree of Life." He grasped my hands tightly. "They are burying her today. Are you going to Norway House?"

"No, I'm staying here with you."

By his bed was a beautiful black and white photograph of Aurelia, newly wed, in a stylish suit and hat and by her side their first son, Vernon, in a white sailor suit.

Lori and Chief Eric Apetagon stopped by to visit Edward. They were a pleasant young couple. To me, Chief Apetagon said, "I've heard a lot about you. If you taught Edward in grade 3, you must be 104!"

"Close," I replied. We all laughed.

A fine lady from Cross Lake also came to visit—Rebecca, the school's coordinator, who told me she'd obtained her degree in education from the University of Manitoba. The patient in the bed next to Edward's called over, "I've been listening. What an interesting life you lead, Edward!"

At one point, Edward asked me to massage his hands and shoulders with lotion. The doctor had told him he needed to turn over regularly, but no one came to help him. It took every ounce of his energy to pull himself over, using the bed railing. I realized that the skin was rubbing off his shoulders. I saw the racist treatment of First Nations patients with my own eyes and ears in the hospital. When I asked at the nurses' desk if Edward could have an air mattress to make him more comfortable, due to his bedsore, the clerk said it would take two weeks to get one. I asked if Edward's name was already on the list.

"No, it's not."

"Could you put it on, please?"

"Yes, I suppose."

When I phoned my sister Kae, who is a nurse, she was disgusted about Edward's bedsore. No one should have a bedsore in this day and age, she told me.

That evening, some of Edward's family arrived to share news of Aurelia's funeral. When I got up to leave, Edward said, "You don't need to leave when people come. You are family, too."

Early on Sunday morning, my Winnipeg friends Mary and Karl Starodub took me to their Catholic church. The congregation sang one of my favourite hymns, the "Ode to Joy." My friend dedicated her mass to Edward. That afternoon, I had another visit with Edward. He was happy to see me, and we had some quiet talks. He thanked me for coming to Winnipeg to be by his side. "There's no place I'd rather be," I replied.

After a while, he asked me to help him move his table closer and to put his wheelchair somewhere else. When I couldn't get things shifted around to suit him, he said, "Sometimes I wonder about you." Then came his irresistible laugh.

In the months to come, whenever I got muddled up with something or I couldn't find my pen or my glasses, I'd look at Edward's portrait in its silver frame and in my mind hear him say again, "Sometimes I wonder about you." I'd laugh, and he seemed so close.

When the dietician asked Edward what he'd like to eat, he said, "Native steroids." She looked puzzled. Edward said, "Macaroni."

Svetlana, a spiritual worker, came and talked to Edward. His Brazilian nurse talked to me. When I explained to him who Edward was, the nurse said he had heard of the shocking residential schools. He also said Edward needed to get out of bed more.

The day after this, two physiotherapists came to get Edward up. He had to tell them how to lift him and put him in his wheelchair. Then one of them said to me, "You'll be here?"

"Yes."

They left then, saying to call them when Edward was tired.

Edward exclaimed, "I'm human again! I can look out the window! I can't remember when I last sat up." We chatted and talked about old times.

Finally he said, "I guess you should call them. I'm getting tired."

Edward and I had become rather well known through our CBC interview and the *United Church Observer* article, and one afternoon a young man, Marc-Yvan Hébert, came to the hospital to ask if he could make a documentary about us for CBC/Radio-Canada. Edward and I agreed, because we wanted our story to be told.

At the same time, Patrick White from the *Globe and Mail* contacted us to see if we would be willing to be interviewed.

Edward and I discussed the topics we wanted to talk about in advance. We agreed on three very important points. At one point, he covered his eyes and cried as he told me about his testimony before the residential school compensation board.

"I couldn't remember what Mr. S. looked like," he said. "I took my older cousin Albert with me to describe Mr. S. at my testimony."

Edward was tired, and soon he dropped off. I sat beside him, letting him sleep. As I reflected on how we had arrived here together and our friendship, I knew that a sacred force was at work, and I was thankful.

Chapter 28

Florence's Story: A Voice Would Speak to Me

Edward continued to have difficult times in the hospital. When a nurse came to change the dressing on the ulcer on his lower back, it was such a painful procedure that he cried out. The hospital still had no air mattress for him, but he was apparently next on the list.

As part of the documentary about us, CBC/Radio-Canada wanted to film me on Friday, June 18, down at the Forks in Winnipeg, where opening ceremonies were being held for the first national event of the Truth and Reconciliation Commission. We went to the building where the healing circles were being held. People could sign up if they wished to speak, which I did. Others could sit outside the circle, as Marc-Yvan did. I sat where cameraman Scott Prouse was satisfied with his camera position. I realized I'd be second-last to speak.

Before survivors began to speak, helpers in red shirts gave each of us a small reddish stone from Pipestone and a fragment of tobacco. The helpers moved around the inner circle, smudging each of us with an eagle feather. Lastly, each of us was given a small paper cup of water.

A huge buffalo hide lay in the middle of the circle. On it was a large, rectangular cedar box, intricately carved and painted. On the wider side, facing me, was a brown face topped by white hair, tears streaming from closed eyes, mouth slightly turned down. In the background were green and black diagonal lines and a buffalo horn. The box exuded a powerful message. Its lid lay at the side. We were told this was the memory box, and we were all invited to put significant objects into it.

A Blackfoot leader from Alberta gave the introduction, and his wife sang a song. Justice Murray Sinclair, the TRC chairperson, sat quietly, holding a thin black notebook and a pen.

One of the earliest speakers was the son of Bernie Lee. Mr. Lee had become the principal at Norway House Residential School after I left. His son told us how he had lived in the school dormitory with the First Nations boys. His statement was positive, and he put his grey, red-trimmed residential school blanket into the memory box. All the other statements were horrific and painful; many brought tears to my eyes. We had started at 3 p.m., and by about 5:00 we were only halfway through. One woman sang a water song as we all stood up. Justice Sinclair told us he would hear every survivor and encouraged us to be respectful of the time we used.

Then it was my turn. I apologized on behalf of my English ancestors who had harmed them. "I have gone through a personal truth and reconciliation with one of my former students, Edward Gamblin," I said. I rose and walked over to the memory box. As I placed one of Edward's *Cree Road* CDs inside, I said, "On it he sings 'Survivor's Voice.'" My voice broke and tears clouded my eyes. Helpers came to comfort me, and one gave me another cup of water. Many people clapped after I finished speaking.

The last man in the circle could not speak for some time, but he finally took the plunge and gave his statement, a tragic story he'd never told anyone before. It was 7 p.m., and we were finished.

Justice Murray Sinclair rose to end the circle. He told us he'd been in many such circles, but this one was exceptional. Then he

Jack Beardy was in Florence's first class at Norway House.

turned to me and said, "We all know Edward Gamblin. You should all read this morning's *Globe and Mail.* Florence and Edward's story is very well told there." I was touched.

When two women from across the circle came and hugged me, I said to them, "I love you." Justice Sinclair told us to express this to one another. He said it will take seven generations to heal if we work hard at helping our children.

Out in the hall, a man in a wheelchair asked me when I'd been at Norway House. When I said I'd been Miss Pockett then, the man almost shouted, "Miss Pockett, I'm Jack Beardy." I gave him a hug. He'd been in my first class in 1954 and was from Split Lake.

"I remember you were excited about Santa Claus coming," I told him.

His wife smiled. "He still is."

I went back and told Edward all about it. He said he'd write Justice Sinclair a note.

The next day Marc and Scott from Radio-Canada came to interview Edward in his hospital room. Edward was wearing a black Native Pride cap and the stunning blue satin ribbon shirt his daughter had brought for him, trimmed with white, turquoise, yellow and red ribbons around the cuffs, on the shoulders and at the neck. He looked handsome.

When Marc asked Edward what it was like when he first went to residential school, Edward said he had felt really scared. "I had to deal with people I didn't know. I didn't know the language they spoke. They had a different culture. I purposely got into trouble in school so I would have to stay after school. We tried to keep back from that experience in the playroom. Later, I had to look for the real Edward, as I had been stripped of my identity. I had to find where he was. A voice would speak to me, saying, 'You are Cree, Native, not an assimilated white person.'"

I was proud, as always, of my student.

Edward had many visitors over the next few days. I was booked to fly home to Courtenay soon, and my heart ached. I didn't know how I was going to leave him. He was very ill, and I prayed for him. I wondered fearfully if he would ever go home from the hospital.

Marc-Yvan Hébert's CBC documentary included many charming pictures of a happy little Edward. There was also the picture of Aurelia and Edward taken by me in the church where they were married and one of the three of us down at the old Hudson's Bay Fort gate. The documentary, titled *On the Road to Reconciliation*, explained that Edward had become a popular western singer, and there was a picture of Ray St. Germain announcing that this year's inductee for the Lifetime Achievement Award for Music was Edward Gamblin. Unfortunately, Edward never saw the film because he passed away before it aired on November 28, 2010.

Chapter 29 🖋

Florence's Story: "Later." "Later."

On the day I was scheduled to fly home from Winnipeg, my friend Mary drove me to the Health Sciences Centre for a final visit with Edward. He was busy, with company coming and going. Some had important business to talk to him about, including residential school student compensation, and it appeared he was going to be successful. Down in the cafeteria, I had what had become my favourite lunch: a sandwich, a date-filled cookie and coffee. I sat at a round table in the vaulted entranceway and watched the passing people: an elder being pushed in a wheelchair clutching his belongings, grannies arriving with children neatly dressed. Some stopped to shop at the concession, picking up gifts and flowers to take to patients.

When I returned to Edward's room with the coffee he had ordered, he showed me Aurelia's memorial bulletin. He recited part of a song he'd written for his mother that also appeared in the bulletin for Aurelia, "Lovely Flowers."

> They placed a Bible in your hand
> All kinds of flowers around you
> And that soft sweet smile on your face
> Takes me back to the day I first saw you.

It's so hard holdin' back the tears
With the children standing around you
And it's hard to see you layin' there
With these lovely flowers around you.

Edward was shattered by losing Aurelia and not being able to be at her memorial. In a song dedicated to her, he'd written, "My world would end without you." He drifted off to sleep for a while, and when he awoke I softly said, "I have to go now."

"Oh yes."

I hugged him. "I hope you'll be better soon. Son, I love you."

As I began to cry, Edward comforted me. "Don't worry about me. It will be all right." He gave me Kleenex to wipe my tears, to comfort me.

"Later."

"Later," I replied.

I turned, crying, and walked out of his room, down the hall, out of ward GD4, to the elevator, down through the lobby and out the front door.

As I flew back over the prairies, home of the Cree and Big Bear, I looked down as usual at all the sections of land and adjoining roads that stretched as far as the eye could see. Edward's people, who now live mostly on reserves, once freely roamed this land without the restrictions of our borders and fences.

At the Comox Airport, Glenn, my beloved first son, was there to meet me. I was back in another world now, far away from my fourth son, whom I also deeply loved.

Chapter 30

Florence's Story: The Owl

It was strange to be back home again. I walked in my garden and talked to my flowers. Cleaned off the back deck. Thought of how immaculate but welcoming everything had been in my friend Mary's house and yard in Winnipeg. When I checked my email, there was a message from her. She wanted me to send her updates on Edward. She was praying for him.

When I went over to my second son Ian's place, my grandsons Noah and Ethan were sitting on the sidewalk waiting for me. They looked so excited to see me, running to me for hugs and saying, "I love you." When I got back to my house in the evening, I felt very lonely, my head ringing. The clock said 12:12 a.m. It was a number my husband Gerd would have liked, being such a mathematician. I went out to the far end of my deck where I could see the moon, and I felt Gerd's presence for a brief second.

The next day was June 26. On that day six years earlier, we'd held a gathering of friends and family in our backyard to honour Gerd's memory. Ian and Glenn had carried our blue canoe to the podium with my grandsons Owen and Noah sitting in it, pounding their paddles on the gunnels as a welcome to all present, a First Nations tradition.

When I got home from lunch with my family, the phone was ringing.

"This is your son Edward." He sounded great. "I'm feeling better. The nurses had been overmedicating me. Before, I was very confused."

I was elated. But when I phoned Edward the next morning, he was hiccuping and coughing. "I'm running out of breath," he told me. The next day was rough for Edward too. He sounded worn out, lacking energy. I was very worried.

Over the next two weeks, Edward and I stayed in touch by phone. I spoke to some of his family, too; things were difficult for them with the death of their mother and with their father in hospital in Winnipeg. I took a day trip with a friend to BC's west coast on July 14, and just as we were about to start back to Courtenay, my cell phone rang. It was Edward, phoning from the hospital. He sounded fine, his voice strong and clear. I was greatly encouraged. He's going to make it, I thought. He'll work on those two CDs he has planned.

At 5:26 the following morning, Edward called again. He thanked me for everything I'd done. Apologized for waking me. He said, "I feel better. No hiccups. It makes me feel alive." Hallelujah! I emailed Ruby, one of his former teachers, to share the good news.

Many people had read Patrick White's *Globe and Mail*[1] article "Together they've turned shame into pride." When I talked to Edward about it, he said, "I've read our article fifty times." I too reread it. The opening paragraph was enticing. "This truth and reconciliation commission consists of two people, a hospital room and some tear-jerking country twang. They have overcome 2,000 kilometres of geography and 150 years of troubled history to join, hand to latex glove, mother to adopted son."

It finished with Edward saying, "I cherish her company, otherwise I would be very lonely right now. This here is reconciliation on a one-to-one basis. That's the only way healing can work."

While preparing to pray at my big oak tree as I did every evening, I looked up into its branches and saw a barred wing and then a dark face with small ears, almost like a cat's. The creature looked at me for a long time as I talked softly to it. It was an owl. I thanked it for being in my garden. Later, I came to believe that, too soon, the owl had come to call Edward's name.

Chapter 31

Florence's Story: Flowers Around You

Edward died in hospital on July 27, just a month after he had called to tell me he felt so alive. Stricken with grief, I flew to Norway House, accompanied by my sister Lorna.

July 30, 2010, a day I'll never forget, started simply enough. In the lobby of the York Boat Inn, there was a Manitoba map showing all of the province's reserves with their First Nations names. A numbered chart gave the English translations. I'd decided I'd like to own a copy, and the desk clerk suggested I check at the band office. Lorna and I walked the short distance to the office, where we were warmly welcomed, but no one had such a map. We stayed to admire the elegant band council chambers, dominated by a huge round black table, black leather chairs and four immense paintings of sweeping northern scenes by Gayle Sinclair. Around the outside of the chamber were historical photographs and paintings by other local artists, including four impressive ones by Edward Gamblin. I inquired if there was any possibility that one of the paintings could be displayed on Edward's memory table in the church for his funeral, and the staff person said she'd look into it.

When Lorna and I returned to the Inn, Angelique phoned to say she'd pick me up. We stopped first at Janice's house, where I picked up my beautiful red and white wreath made of paper roses. We talked for a few minutes in Janice's kitchen about how Aurelia and Edward had taken her in when she was a troubled teenager. She thought of them as Mom and Dad, and she missed both of them.

As we drove to the airport, Edward's songs played constantly on NCI FM radio and the local station. Condolences poured in from people all over the province. Edward's coffin was set to arrive on that day's flight from Winnipeg.

There were what seemed like hundreds of cars and trucks parked around the airport terminal. People stood talking, comforting each other. Chief Eric Apetagon came to greet me and shake my hand. I visited with a group of children near a spot with a view out onto the tarmac. From there, I could see the airport's flagpole: the Canadian flag on top, the Manitoba flag below. Both were flying at half-mast.

We heard the familiar sound of the shiny white Perimeter Air plane as it circled, then landed. Passengers disembarked as anguished mourners moved out toward the plane. Eight pallbearers walked single-mindedly toward the back cargo door. I could no longer hold back the flood of tears locked within me. Edward's cousin, Christopher Ross, held me and cried too. "I've lost my brother," he wept.

When Edward's pine coffin appeared, decorated with burned-in designs, it was gently lowered into the outstretched hands of the pallbearers.

Edward, I despaired, how must you feel arriving home like this? There should be a cheering, hand-waving, whistling crowd here to welcome you as you stride off the plane, conquering hero and man of wisdom. You, a person who overcame sexual and physical abuse in residential schools to become a social worker, a writer, a musician and a spokesperson for your people. But no. A large woman in a gold shirt put her strong arms around me.

The pallbearers proceeded slowly to the waiting, ivory-coloured hearse. The funeral procession headed slowly away from the airport, led by the flashing lights of a police car. Cars and trucks filled with family and friends reverently followed. I rode with a young woman, Loretta, who had also been brought up by Edward and Aurelia. What a large extended family knew their support and caring! My driver's radio was on, and we heard hymns and message after message of condolence come over the wires for the Gamblin family. My escort sang along in a beautiful strong voice. Her faith and peacefulness gave me comfort.

The lace-draped hearse parked in the driveway beside Edward's family home. Pallbearers opened the back door, and Edward's coffin was drawn partway out. A small group gathered around, including his family and two ministers who read scripture and recited prayers. Fifty barked and ran back and forth. I was sure he knew Edward was there and was distressed, so I petted him and tried to console him.

With Edward's coffin back in the hearse the funeral procession wound past the settlement of Rossville to Keenanow United Church on Norway House's historic point on Little Playgreen Lake. Edward's coffin rested on a bench in the hall. The head end of his casket was open, with a white lace cloth draped to frame his face. He lay peacefully, wearing the blue ribbon shirt Aurelia had made for him and his signature cap.

On the wall behind his casket hung a large white cloth with a picture of Jesus on it. Around the picture were fastened many-coloured paper flowers. Beautiful wreaths, including my red and white one, stood at the foot of the casket.

Quietly, I joined family and friends sitting in a large circle. Three men were playing guitars and singing hymns, mostly in Cree. Someone passed me a black hymn book, and I joined in the singing. There was a familiar rhythm and strength to the trio's playing. Had Edward's music influenced them, or had his music captured the traditional Cree sound?

Edward's distraught family stayed by his casket for a long time. Others filed by—friends and associates. As I stood and looked at Edward, I talked to him for the last time. As I started to cry, he seemed to give me a great big smile.

After the viewing, I walked the short distance back to the York Boat Inn. After supper at the restaurant with Lorna, I crashed into bed. I woke in a panic, jotting down some ideas for Edward's eulogy.

The next evening Lorna and I decided to walk up to Church Point. When I arrived, we realized that another part of Edward's wake was in progress. We stood on the church steps before going in, talking to various people. A tall man in a blue velour suit said to me, "I can't get up the steps. How can I go and see my brother? We played such good rock and roll music together." The man seemed disoriented, and I stood beside him, not knowing what to do. But soon two men came to help him up the steps and into the hall.

Inside, we paused to study the photographs and cards on Edward's memory table. People were singing hymns again, and Edward's family gathered around his casket. Soon a man stepped forward and began to speak as the hall fell silent. I'd read about First Nations orators, and this man was one. He motioned with his hand to Edward, then turned and spoke to everyone. Most of what he said was in Cree, but I could tell his words were powerful. Once in a while he spoke in English. He said that Edward was a quiet man whose silences meant a lot, a storyteller and a spirit with gifts, and that for Edward the gates of heaven had swung wide open.

Chapter 32

Florence's Story: Reverent Drums

Back at the Inn, I worked again on my eulogy for Edward.

"You should go to bed," Lorna said.

"No, I have to finish it tonight."

So she bore with me, and we soldiered on until I was satisfied.

I placed a bookmark in my diary at the page where I would begin Edward's eulogy. I would hold my treasured feather to give me courage.

Edward's funeral was set for 2:00 the next afternoon. Lorna and I walked together the short distance to the church. Outside the door someone handed us bulletins. On the front were words from Isaiah 40:31:

Those who hope in the Lord
Will renew their strength.
They will soar
On wings like eagles.
They will run and not grow weary.
They will walk
And not be faint.

Edward's daughter Jane said softly, "I like these words. They mean so much."

"I do, too," I told her.

"I imagine him hunting, dancing, running like the wind in the Creator's beautiful new world now, no more pain or sorrow," Jane continued.

The pallbearers placed Edward's casket at the front of the church. After the opening prayers and hymn, Jane read a poem, controlling her broken heart to do it well. The poem, "A Daddy's Love," was moving and spoke of the love and laughter they had shared. "A father's touch, a daddy's kiss," she read. "A grieving daughter, you're greatly missed."

Chief Eric Apetagon sang the second hymn, accompanying himself on his guitar. And then it was time to give Edward's eulogy. I carried the eagle feather he'd given me to keep me calm. I spoke of how I had met Edward as a child and how in recent years he had become a son to me. "We had many wonderful laughs together," I said. "There was never a dull moment being with him. He talked about his past, his present and his future. He never hesitated to speak his mind, because he spoke for his people, his family, and his grandchildren. He told me how the residential school had erased his culture. But Edward went searching for it through many ceremonies and teachings. Once he walked from Norway House to Ottawa to support residential school survivors.

"Edward was a gifted man who willingly shared his wisdom and many talents. He was an exceptional writer, writing many songs, poems and letters. He even began to write a book about his residential school experiences. The first chapter begins: 'My mind goes back to days I wish I had not known.'

"Edward was also a talented painter, and many of his works of art are displayed in public spaces here in Norway House.

"After finishing grade 12, Edward attended the University of Manitoba to become a social worker. He dedicated himself to helping others at Child Services in Winnipeg and as a treatment counsellor in Edmonton at the Night Wind Centre. He was the coordinator for Thunder Bear Healing Lodge, where he worked with people fighting addictions.

"Today, as I watched the ivory-coloured hearse bearing his body and flying the Canadian flag make its way to this church I thought of Edward's lyrics in 'Survivor's Voice': 'Why just me? Canada! Heal with me.' He explained these words to me once. He said, 'I am not the only one who needs to heal. So do the perpetrators, all the rest of Canadians must heal also.' Here's to the hope that one day soon, we as a country can heal together.'"

After the closing prayer, I moved slowly outside into the sunshine, carrying my feather. People stood in groups talking, then gathered in cars to follow the funeral procession. Lorna and I were invited into a large van with many others, very much part of this occasion.

We drove away from the arresting, familiar view of Norway House, down a slight incline, past the small community of Rossville, and finally out into the sparsely populated area where the road led to Northend Cemetery. It was a time of reflection. My mind went back to days long, long ago, when I had first come to teach at Norway House and seen the tiny little boy in the new United Church Indian Residential School.

Many people had arrived before us. We parked and walked over to where the pallbearers were slowly lowering Edward's coffin into the ground. I kept my "feather of courage" with me.

Each of us cast in coloured paper roses taken from the cloth around the picture of Jesus at the church, and then strong men shovelled clods of earth into Edward's tomb, where he lay beside Aurelia.

The drummers at the gravesite. Mike, Edward's brother, is second from the right.

As Reverend Evelyn Broadfoot read to us, I thought of the time when Edward had read the Bible for himself. The Saviour was with you while Mr. S. beat you, Edward, I thought, and he was with you every day through every struggle all your life.

Two men began to reverently drum. One was Edward's brother Mike. His drum was painted with a lone loon, looking for a lost mate as it swam through the marsh. There was silence, except for the gentle, intense, slow drumming.

A large white floral guitar was placed on Edward's grave. Did I also hear a distant guitar strumming, small moccasined feet dancing, joyous youthful shouts and whoops of celebration and an audience responding?

It was over. People were going to their cars, driving away. I paused by Edward's peaceful resting place for a few minutes, holding my feather. I wondered if I would ever return to this sacred place. My heart was broken.

Epilogue

God gave Edward Gamblin many gifts, one of them being the gift of love. Edward loved his wife, Aurelia, and his children, his people and, yes, even me, a residential school teacher.

In the residential school Edward and the other children were forced to say the Lord's Prayer, to assimilate and to be like their oppressors. But Edward found there was another way, even though he was a Christian. He sought his own Cree people's spirituality, his culture, his Creator and the Healing Circle.

"Did He give me the gift of Voice so some could silence me?" Edward asks in his music. But through his music and art, and love, Edward Gamblin found his voice. He cried out and told the world about his abuse and suffering, but he did not blame. With his gift of compassion, he forgave his perpetrators. He forgave and called out, "Canada, heal with me."

And Edward's people are healing today as they relate their stories to the Truth and Reconciliation Commission, some for the first time. Many couldn't tell their parents, grandparents, siblings or partners what had happened to them. But in the loving, healing circle of fellow survivors they unburden themselves and perhaps take the first step to recovery.

Operational History of Norway House Indian Residential School

Courtesy of the United Church of Canada Archives
Researched and written by Ruth Taylor and Susan Roy, 2013

Dates of operation:

1900–1946

1952–1965

Operated by:

The Methodist Missionary Society and, after 1925, by the Board of Home Missions of the United Church.

Location:

In central Manitoba on approximately forty acres of Norway House Reserve No. 17, at Rossville. The reserve is on the shores of Little Playgreen Lake, about forty kilometres north of Lake Winnipeg.

> We spent many hours out-of-school with the children—planning and carrying out special events, teaching Sunday school, leading groups such as Mission Band, Explorers, and C.G.I.T. [Canadian Girls in Training]. We took turns leading morning chapel. I loved taking the children on field trips in the surrounding bush—they taught me so much about the environment that was so familiar to them. Often we built a fire and toasted marshmallows.
>
> —Margaret Anne Reid recalls her two years as a young teacher at Norway House.[1]

Establishment

In 1840, Reverend James Evans, of the Methodist Church, established a mission at Norway House, on Little Playgreen Lake in
central Manitoba. Just across the bay was a Hudson's Bay Company post, a regional hub that collected furs from the company's
extensive Manitoba network and sent them on to York Factory
on Hudson Bay for export. Swampy Cree families of the region,
many of whom worked as trappers and shippers for the HBC,
were drawn to Norway House as well, and by the 1860s they had
a large and prosperous settlement there.[2]

However, the introduction of steamships on the Red River
and Lake Winnipeg redirected goods away from York Factory and
soon led to Norway House's decline in the regional trade network.
Facing resource depletion as well, the Norway House community,
whose lands would not serve for farming, petitioned for a reserve
farther south. Together with other Cree people of the area they
sought a treaty with the federal government.

Treaty 5, negotiated in 1875 with the Cree and Saulteaux
nations living around Lake Winnipeg, established reserves; pay-
ments of annuities; distribution of agricultural equipment and
medical supplies; the continued right to hunt, fish and trap on
lands covered by the treaty; and education.[3] As part of the agreement, an initial group of some two hundred Norway House people relocated to Fisher River, on the southeastern shore of Lake
Winnipeg, but many others remained on the reserve established
at Little Playgreen Lake.

Reverend Evans had opened a day school for about twenty-
five students at Norway House soon after he established his
mission, with the aim of teaching the children to read both English and their own Indigenous languages.[4] However, it was not
until 1898 that the Methodist Church requested funds from the
federal government to build a boarding school at the location.

The residence would serve the numerous Aboriginal communities in the region, many of whom did not wish to send their children as far away as Brandon Indian Residential School, in southern Manitoba. The Department of Indian Affairs (DIA) approved funds toward construction of a residence and a per capita grant of seventy-five dollars to a maximum of fifty students.[5]

The residence opened in the fall of 1900 with a staff of three and took in fifty-six boarders its first year. As part of their vocational training, the boys cut wood, fetched the school's water from the lake, tended the vegetable garden and helped in the kitchen and with baking. "As they are mostly small, they are really unable to do very heavy work," wrote the school's first principal, E.F. Hardiman.[6] The girls were taught plain and fancy sewing, dressmaking, baking, ironing and washing. They also performed other housework and did all the mending. In later years, the boys cared for the school's cattle and learned some carpentry.

The children took their academic classes in the day school along with fifty to sixty day students from the local community, a situation that led to overcrowding in the classroom and overwork for the lone schoolteacher.[7] After a schoolroom was built for the residence in 1903, senior students took their classes there, but the junior residents continued to attend the day school.[8] By that time, the boarding school staff numbered six.

Fire, 1913

By 1910, the Norway House residence was in bad repair, and school officials began to look for a new site to rebuild. A DIA surveyor sent to assess the situation was taken aback by the state of the building. He reported that the cellar was flooded and the building had poor insulation, but most serious was the risk of fire: "There is a continuous draft between the walls and were a fire to start the whole thing would be in flames in a few minutes. As the windows in the sleeping dormitories are barred I do not see how the children could be saved. The danger is great as no less than 13 stoves are in use in different parts of the building in winter."[9]

Despite this warning and despite the Norway House band's surrender in 1910 of forty acres of its reserve at Rossville as a school site, construction of a new building was postponed. On February 26, 1913, as predicted, the school burned to the ground in a fire started by a wood-burning stove. Luckily, according to reports, there were no injuries or lives lost. The resident students, who numbered around fifty, continued to receive classes, billeted in local homes, the empty hospital and the HBC store until a new residence could be constructed.[10]

That building, designed to accommodate eighty students, opened on October 15, 1915. Ninety-two students were enrolled in the first year.[11]

Student Recruitment

Initially, recruitment of students for Norway House Indian Residential School (IRS) focused on Norway House itself and the surrounding but still remote communities of Cross Lake, God's Lake, Oxford House, Island Lake, Poplar River and Berens River. In later years, however, dissatisfaction with the boarding school in a number of these communities forced recruiters to seek students from farther afield, in particular Nelson House, Split Lake and Fox Lake, but also the very distant communities of Churchill, Shamattawa and Trout Lake, Ontario.[12]

The school's second principal, Rev. J.A. Lousley, was a particularly keen recruiter, which may in part explain his frequent absences from the school. Although the residence was built for eighty students, he worked to reach an enrollment of one hundred.[13] As a result, the school was overcrowded (in 1916, students were sleeping two to a bed), and the day school was saddled with absorbing the students who could not fit into the boarding school's two classrooms.[14] The children's health suffered, and provisions of food and clothing were sometimes insufficient.[15] Under Lousley's successors, authorized enrollment increased even further, to one hundred in 1922 and 105 in 1923. And in 1925, the school petitioned the DIA, unsuccessfully, to increase enrollment to 110.[16]

Conditions at Norway House led at least one community to withdraw its children from the school altogether. In the winter of 1915–16, nine children from Berens River arrived home showing signs of frostbite and complaining that they had been fed rotten fish.[17] When Chief Jacob Berens accused the school of breach of contract and refused to send more children until conditions had improved, Lousley rebuked him: "You have long hindered the children of your people from attending these great schools that God has provided for your people...So I, one of the men God has sent to you people in this North Land, call you to repent of this your wrong doing before it is too late."[18] In his reply, Berens wrote, "I am glad I will eventually be judged by a higher judge than yourself," and severed all ties to the school until Lousley was removed—which he was, in July of that year.[19]

Children generally travelled to Norway House by canoe, even when air travel, which the DIA considered too expensive, became available. Travel to Island Lake—not the most distant of the communities—took eight days, exposing the children "to the possibility of wet weather and colds" and leaving them in poor shape to start school, according to Principal R.T. Chapin.[20] Travel to and from the school also ate up a good part of the children's two-month summer holiday. However, when administrators in 1935 complained, the DIA proposed simply keeping the children at school year-round.[21] Eventually, children were flown in, with a teacher escort, on Norseman bush planes.[22]

Discipline and Truancy

From the outset, the school administration found truancy a problem. Principal Hardiman, who lasted only a year in his post, asked the DIA to enforce attendance: "I urge the necessity of bringing into operation laws that will enable the Principal of this school to be supreme in his work in the school, and not to be openly defied by certain members of the Band without having the least chance of redress."[23] Eight years later, after noting that thirteen students were absent "because of some paltry notion of either the child or its guardian," Principal Lousley made a similar plea.[24]

The insistence on retaining at Norway House IRS children who were considered difficult or unhappy led to some of the more serious incidents of abuse reported there. In the winter of 1906–7, Charles Clyne ran away from the residence after a staff member punished him for wetting his bed and for allegedly stealing clothing. Clyne spent the night in a cabin in the bush with the result that both his feet froze and he was permanently disabled. During the subsequent investigation, Lousley admitted to having thrashed the boy himself many times—more than any other student. Lousley contended that Clyne "deserved all he received as he was the very worst pupil in the school."[25]

The investigating inspector, in contrast, argued that a student considered "undesirable" should have been given an early dismissal. In addition, the inspector concluded that the principal, who was often away, should take a more direct role in the supervision of his staff and the school in general; that the school should have made more of an effort to find the boy after he went missing; and that bedwetting should have received medical attention rather than punishment—a solution, the inspector added, that "might have been more in accordance with Christian methods."[26]

The school's methods were questioned a second time in 1915, after the new residence opened, when Lousley had a boy tied up in order to prevent him running away. R.T. Ferrier, of the Methodist Missionary Society, defended the principal's actions, arguing that "this was the only time that this was done, and it was during a time that the ice was rotten in the bay and they were afraid that his foolishness might lead him to run away over the ice, and thus lose his life."[27] Again, the investigating inspector recommended the boy's discharge.[28]

Principals did not always take such a hard line. In 1934, for instance, Reverend W.W. Shoup let an eight-year-old who was "a little inclined to brood for his parents" go with them for the year "to the bush."[29] Shoup, however, had faced other allegations. In 1930, shortly after he became principal, Arthur Felix, father of a fifteen-year-old boy at the school, accused Shoup of striking his son and dragging him to another room where he strapped him. Shoup denied the severity of the assault. The RCMP investigated and the case went to trial in January, at which time the judge dismissed the charge and warned the principal to punish with a strap. The investigating officer noted that since Shoup's appointment the previous summer, he had heard different stories of the principal's harshness toward the pupils.[30]

Reverend Shoup was dismissed in 1934. A letter written in defense of his administration noted, "He has mellowed in his view and actions as time goes on. He now has the goodwill of the community, and of the children—as far as is possible, he being the Principal."[31]

Student Health

Reverend Shoup's supporters credited him with improving the students' health, which had long been a serious problem at the school.[32] In the school's first thirteen years, the rate of reported deaths at the school was 36 per 1000. During the next period for which records exist, 1933 to 1941, it dropped to 7 per 1000.[33] The biggest killer was tuberculosis, the "great white plague," which was rampant in northern First Nations communities. As Dr. E.L. Stone wrote of Norway House Agency in 1925, "Disease here means one malady, and one only, for all practical purposes. That is tuberculosis. Practically nobody dies of anything else."[34] In 1906–7, nine children at Norway House IRS died of the disease.

Epidemics, which swept the school on a regular basis, made health matters worse. Lousley wrote, for example, in 1902, "We have suffered, in common with the reserve upon which we are situated, from a most virulent epidemic of whooping-cough, bronchitis and pneumonia; most suffering from all three diseases at the same time, and in addition, some had chicken pox." Three children died as a result, but Lousley insisted that this "could not be taken to indicate unhealthy conditions in or around the school, as there were about sixty-five deaths on the reserve from the same cause."[35]

Principal Shoup, however, saw room for improvement. "Studying the situation I am assured that the over-crowding of this school in the past accounts for the condition of many." By reducing enrollment from 105 to eighty-nine, Shoup found that "we can maintain what appears to be a more sanitary condition."[36] He promoted outdoor recreation and put the children on the half-day system, with classes in the morning only: "The afternoons are devoted to outdoor exercises. For the boys a course of regular military drill for upwards of one hour—and then football or some other healthful games—all under the Sr. teacher. The girls have been given the regular course of drill taught in Manitoba ordinary Day Schools." [37] Shoup had a children's slide and an outdoor rink built as well.

The presence of a hospital and medical staff in Rossville, sporadically before 1914 and permanently thereafter, may have also contributed to better student survival rates. R.T. Chapin, principal from 1934 to 1941, wrote in his memoirs, "It meant a great deal to us to have a resident doctor, hospital and nurses on the Indian Agency grounds so close to us. It was seldom we had any serious illness, but it was a comfort to know that if the doctor took a boy or girl to the hospital he was receiving the best care possible."[38]

Malnourishment had been a source of concern at the school as well. The problem was particularly acute in 1914–15, just after the new building opened, when administrators were caught without enough food supplies to see them through the winter.[39] After complaints from the children's home communities, the DIA ordered an investigation. Inspector Bunn found that several children who had been brought to the hospital for treatment and "low physical condition" had improved considerably, if not completely, after receiving "proper nourishing food" there. He noted that the school provided little in the way of fatty foods, that the bread was poorly cooked, that they had few root or other vegetables, that two carcasses of beef was all the school had for the entire winter, and that "suckers" had been served at times instead of good fish.[40]

Hope Island Farm

G.F. Denyes, who replaced Reverend Lousley in 1916, appears to have been the first principal to attempt serious farming at Norway House. By 1919, under his direction, thirty of the forty acres on which the school was situated had been cleared (ploughing under the old mission graveyard in the process) and several acres brought under cultivation: "This year we have corn for table use, a good number of tomatoes ripening on the vines and almost every variety of garden produce. We had oats ripen by Aug. 20. We are only able to raise a little compared with what we need. In three years, we have increased our cattle from five to twenty-four. Our hogs from none at that time to twenty-four, sixteen of these are large ones....We had one team then now two and we expect to get another."[41]

In order to increase production further, Denyes started developing land on Hope Island, some ten kilometres across the lake from the residence, as a woodlot and hayfield. His petition to have 571.2 acres there turned over permanently to the school for its use was granted in 1923 by federal order-in-council.[42] In later years, Hope Island served as pasturage as well. Principal Shoup increased the dairy herd.[43] And in 1942, Principal Caldwell introduced goats and instructed students in their care and feed.[44] Though it was no longer farmed, Hope Island still served in the 1960s as a site for student camping trips.[45]

Curriculum

Vocational instruction at Norway House IRS appears to have been limited, in the case of boys, to carpentry (they built the school's outbuildings) and farming for the school's food. These chores came to occupy so much of the children's time, however, that in 1923 the Indian Agent complained that they were spending too much time outdoors, building fences and breaking new ground: "Pupils under the age of 16 at least, or Grade 6 or even 7, should have at least half day classroom work."[46] Student labour, however, was crucial to the school's operation. In 1934 Principal Shoup asked permission to keep children who had reached the age of sixteen in school just to help run the place: "Up to sixteen the pupil is not able to be of any very marked assistance with the regular work of the school except for lighter tasks. During the years from sixteen to eighteen we find the pupils are able to carry our [sic] heavier tasks and so take the place of help that would have to be hired from the outside."[47]

Both school administrators and DIA officials were aware that the skills taught at Norway House IRS were not the ones students would most need once they left the school. In direct contrast to Reverend Shoup's proposal to keep students longer, Indian Agent P.G. Lazenby proposed discharging boys at the age of fourteen so they could return home and learn how to make a living: "Boys cannot learn to hunt and trap and fish at school, and these are the only means of earning a living in this country."[48] Similarly, in 1935,

Principal Chapin allowed eight boys to go trap muskrats with men from the community as "they would thus get good instruction in the methods of trapping, which is, after all, what they will depend upon for their living after they leave school."[49]

In an attempt to secure boy students just such a future, in 1942 the school reached an agreement with the Hudson's Bay Company in which the company pledged to hire Norway House IRS graduates. Although the company preferred boys who had reached seventeen or eighteen years of age, it was willing to hire them at sixteen.[50]

The situation of girls was perceived differently. At sixteen, school administrators thought them too young for hospital work, domestic service or marriage and sought to keep them a year or two longer at the school.[51]

Second Fire, 1946

On May 29, 1946, the school building was consumed by a fire that had started in the furnace room. Thanks to the efforts of two boys who woke them and helped them down the fire escape pillars, all the children and the staff escaped safely.[52]

Ruby Beardy provided the following account of the fire, as told to her by her husband, Donald Beardy, one of the heroes that night:

> The fire started at 2:30 during the night. Donald was awakened by a burning sensation in his nose. When he opened his eyes, the dormitory was filled with smoke. Donald jumped out of his bed and ran towards the window which had been partially open. He pushed the screen out and looked down onto the ground. He could see flames gushing out from the wood bin in the furnace room. Instinctively, he woke up his friend, Oliver

Sinclair, who was sleeping in the bed next to his. Oliver leaped up and obediently followed Donald's orders. The two young boys quickly woke up everyone, telling each one to make much noise. All the boys began to bang and hit the beds. They did this to wake up the little girls who were sleeping in another dormitory just below their floor. Donald ran out of the dormitory to wake up the boys' supervisor, Mr Organ, who then went and rang the fire alarm. Mr Organ told Donald to go outside and catch the girls as they came flying down the fire escape pillars. Meanwhile, Oliver was catching the boys at their fire escape. Less than a half hour later, all the children were out of the building and secure in the care of local people who had run to the burning building to help.[53]

The children stayed in local homes until they were able to return to their own communities.

In the wake of the fire, the United Church debated whether or not to rebuild. There was growing interest from First Nations communities to have federally supported local day schools on their reserves and growing pressure from within the church to get out of school administration altogether. In the end, however, church officials, pointing to the "pathetically inadequate" state of the day schools, were not convinced that the federal government was serious about giving Aboriginal children an education.[54] The church rebuilt in 1952, with room for 120 students in two dorms housed in separate buildings in order to minimize the risk of fire.[55] The half-day system was abandoned.

By 1964, there were 138 children in residence at Norway House IRS and 242 day students who lived in their own homes in the community.[56] Margaret Ann Reid recalled her experiences as a young teacher of the grade 2/3 class: "Progress was slow for many of the children—this was partly due to the language barrier—schoolwork was in English—the students were accustomed to talking and thinking in Cree. There were no restrictions on speaking Cree outside the classroom." Reid also noted that attendance continued to be very fluid in the school, as children frequently stayed home to care for siblings or to accompany their families on trapping and fishing excursions.[57]

School Closure

In December 1965, the Hudson's Bay Presbytery of the United Church agreed to have the Board of Home Missions negotiate with the government for the closure of Norway House IRS at the earliest possible date. Under the UCC proposal, the residence was to be converted to classroom space for the day school, and the day school was to be administered by the federal government for Indian children of any Christian denomination.[58] Indian Affairs closed the residence June 30, 1967.

Norway House Indian Residential School Timeline of Operations

Courtesy of the United Church of Canada Archives

Researched and written by Ruth Taylor and Susan Roy, 2013

1840   Reverend James Evans of the Methodist Church establishes Rossville Mission at Norway House, Manitoba, and soon opens a day school for the Cree children there.

1875   The Cree and Salteaux nations living around Lake Winnipeg negotiate Treaty 5 with the federal government, which establishes reserves at Norway House and other locations.

1898   The Methodist Church asks the government for funds to build a boarding school at Rossville. The Department of Indian Affairs funds the school's construction and approves seventy-five dollars per capita to a maximum of fifty students.

1899   The residence opens in the fall with fifty-six boarders and a staff of three. Vocational training consists of cutting wood, fetching water from the lake, tending the garden, cooking, baking, sewing, washing and ironing. Boarders attend the day school along with fifty to sixty day students. The school's first principal, E.F. Hardiman, finds it difficult to enforce attendance.

1902   The school suffers simultaneous epidemics of whooping cough, bronchitis and pneumonia, with some chicken pox as well. Three children die.

1903   A schoolroom for senior students is built for the residence; junior students continue to attend the day school. Staff at the residence numbers six.

1906   During the 1906–7 school year, nine children die from tuberculosis. Student Charles Clyne runs away after being severely punished; his feet freeze and he is permanently disabled. The supervisor who beat him leaves the school and church employment.

1910   The residence building is in poor repair and the threat of fire from the wood-burning stoves is great; school officials decide to rebuild. The Norway House band surrenders forty acres of its reserve as a site for the new residence. Principal Lousley complains of truancy.

1911   On April 1, the DIA and the Methodist Church sign an agreement governing management of the boarding school.

1913   On February 26, the school burns down. The students, who number approximately fifty, continue to receive classes. They are billeted in local homes, the hospital and the HBC store.

1915   The DIA rebuilds the boarding school on the forty acres allocated by the band, a short distance from the old school site. The new building, designed to accommodate eighty boarders, opens October 15. Ninety-two students were enrolled the first year. The school is ill-prepared for so many students. Food and clothing are short, and children show signs of malnourishment. Principal Lousley has a boy tied up to prevent him running away, prompting an investigation by the DIA.

1916   The school is overcrowded; children are sleeping two to a bed. The community of Berens River refuses to send its children back after they arrive home with signs of frostbite and complaining that they have been fed rotten fish. The school has five head of cattle and one team of horses. Principal Lousley is dismissed.

1917   The new principal, George Denyes, begins to expand the school's half-acre garden plot.

1918   A number of children orphaned by the Spanish flu epidemic are taken into the school.

1919   Denyes reports that the boys have cleared thirty of the school's forty acres and have brought several acres under cultivation. They also have twenty-four head of cattle, twenty-four hogs and two teams of horses.

1922   The boundaries of the school property are altered to accommodate a roadway. Enrollment reaches one hundred.

1923   Enrollment is 105. By federal order-in-council, 571.2 acres of Crown land on Hope Island are turned over to the school for its use. The Indian Agent reports that the schoolchildren are spending too much time "building fences and breaking new ground" instead of in the classroom.

1924   The exact boundaries of the lands provided to the school by the Norway House Band are defined.

1925   Management of the school transfers from the Methodist Missionary Society of Canada to the Board of Home Missions of the United Church of Canada. The school petitions the DIA to increase enrollment to 110, but the department refuses.

1930   The RCMP lays charges against Principal Shoup after he uses severe corporal punishment on a boy. The presiding judge dismisses the charges but warns the principal to punish with a strap.

1931   In an attempt to improve student health, Shoup begins to decrease enrollment. He also introduces outdoor exercise drills and has a slide and an outdoor rink built. The school is put on the half-day system, with classes in the morning only.

1933   The school is hit by a whooping cough epidemic when the children return from summer holidays. The disease may have been brought from Oxford House, one of the children's home communities. Shoup increases the dairy herd to provide milk for the students. Enrollment has dropped to eighty-nine.

1934   Principal Shoup asks permission from the DIA to keep students over sixteen in school to help run it. Shoup is dismissed.

1935   The school is quarantined due to an outbreak of chicken pox.

1940   There is an outbreak of typhoid fever, which may have originated in God's Lake.

1942   Principal Caldwell introduces goats. The Hudson's Bay Company signs an agreement, drawn up by the school, to hire Norway House IRS graduates.

1946   On May 29, the school burns down in a fire that starts in the furnace room. With the aid of two boys, students and staff escape safely. The students are billeted in local homes until they can return to their communities. Enrollment is 105.

1948   The DIA begins to survey for the construction of a new building.

1952   The new boarding school, with room for 120 students in residence and two dorms in separate buildings to reduce the risk of fire, reopens in September. Farming ceases and the half-day system is abandoned.

1955   Anglican children who cannot be accommodated by Prince Albert Residential School in Saskatchewan begin to attend Norway House.

1957   Norway House IRS and the Rossville Day School amalgamate.

1964   There are 138 children in residence and another 242 who are day students.

1965   The Executive of the Manitoba Conference agrees to close the school within two years, to give it time to find alternative accommodation for residential students.

1967   On June 30, Norway House IRS closes and the building is converted to a day school classroom. The forty acres assigned to the school revert to Norway House Reserve No. 17. Management of the day school passes to the federal government.

1968   The Crown-owned property on Hope Island is transferred to Manitoba on August 30.

1969   In July, Manitoba takes over the school system at Norway House from the federal government.

Note from the author:

In 1998, the General Council Executive of the United Church formally apologized for its complicity in the system, and the pain and suffering caused by the church's involvement. The full extent of the abuse endured by many residential school students has since become widely known. In addition to their apology, the United Church has published numerous study guides and has established funds to help facilitate ongoing reconciliation.

The Truth and Reconciliation Commission of Canada arose out of the Indian Residential Schools Settlement Agreement, the largest class-action settlement in Canadian history brought forward by former residential school students. The implementation of this agreement began in 2007.

Notes

Preface

1.   Victoria Freeman, *Distant Relations: How My Ancestors Colonized North America* (Toronto: McClelland and Stewart, 2000), 449-450.

Chapter 1

1.   Richard Wagamese, *Dream Wheels* (Toronto: Doubleday Canada, 2006), 391.

Chapter 2

1.   E. Pauline Johnson, "The Song My Paddle Sings" from *Flint and Feather: The Complete Poems of E. Pauline Johnson* (Tekahionwake) (Toronto: Musson, 1930).

Chapter 11

1.   Randy Fred, "Foreword" from *Resistance and Renewal: Surviving the Indian Residential School* by Celia Haig-Brown (Vancouver: Arsenal Pulp Press, 2010), 15-16.

Chapter 21

1.   John Ralston Saul, *A Fair Country: Telling Truths About Canada* (Toronto: Viking, 2008), 17.

2.   Rudy Wiebe, *The Temptations of Big Bear* (Vintage Canada, 1999), 399.

Chapter 23

1.   Richard Wright, "I Remember You. You Were My Teacher" in the *United Church Observer*, May 2009.

Chapter 30

1.   Patrick White, "Together They've Turned Shame into Pride" in the *Globe and Mail*, June 2010.

Operational History of Norway House Indian Residential School

1.   Margaret Anne (Reid) May, "A Northern Adventure: My Adventure at Norway House, Manitoba, August 1957–June 1959," 2007, PP93/3289, United Church of Canada (UCC) Manitoba and N.W. Ontario Conference Archives.

2.   Manitoba. Canada. "Norway House Cree Nation, First Nation No. 278," 2004–2005 First Nations Profiles—MB Region, http://www.gov.mb.ca/conservation/wno/status-report/fa-8.15_norway.pdf.

3.   Kenneth S. Coates, William R. Morrison, Treaties and Historical Research Centre, Indian and Northern Affairs Canada, "Treaty Research Report—Treaty Five (1875)," http://www.aadnc-aandc.gc.ca/eng/1100100028695. Because of the limited potential for agriculture, the reserves at Norway House and other locations were considerably smaller than the reserves established in the prairies.

4.   E.R. Young, The Apostle of the North, Rev. James Evans (Toronto: William

Briggs, 1900), cited in Russell T. Ferrier, Superintendent of Indian Missions, to N.O. Cote, Controller, Land Patents Branch, Feb. 24, 1925, RG10, vol. 6269, file 581-10, Library and Archives Canada (LAC).

5. J.D. McLean, Deputy SGIA, to A. Sutherland, General Secretary, Methodist Missionary Society, Apr. 19, 1898, RG10, vol. 6268, file 581-1, pt. 1, LAC.

6. E.F. Hardiman, principal, to SGIA, June 30, 1902, Department of Indian Affairs (DIA) annual reports, 1902, pp. 305–306.

7. Sutherland to Secretary General of Indian Affairs (SGIA), Dec. 6, 1900, RG10, vol. 6268, file 581-1, pt. 1, LAC.

8. J.A. Lousley, principal, to SGIA, Aug. 8, 1903, DIA annual report, 1903, pp. 336–337; "The Report of Rev. J.A. Lousley, Principal of the Norway House (Methodist) Boarding School, Norway House, Man., for the Year Ended March 31, 1913," DIA annual reports, 1913, pp. 555–556.

9. J.K. McLean, surveyor, to J.D. McLean, Secretary, DIA, Aug. 13, 1910, RG10, vol. 6269, file 581-10, LAC.

10. Ferrier to Secretary, DIA, Mar. 20, 1913, RG10, vol. 6268, file 581-1, pt. 1, LAC.

11. "Norway House Agency," DIA annual reports, 1915, pp. 163–164.

12. For example, Cormie wrote in 1944 regarding school-aged children at Island Lake, "A few used to go to the Norway House School but there are few, if any, going there today." Cormie to George Dorey, Sept. 16, 1944, correspondence, Brandon Residential School, 1938–1953, 509/2/2-5, box J, file 2, UCC Manitoba and N.W. Ontario Conference Archives.

13. J.G. Stewart, Indian Agent, "Monthly Report of the Norway House Boarding School, Apr. 30, 1915," RG10, vol. 6268, file 581-1, pt. 1, LAC. According to the Methodist Church's Superintendent of Missions, Lousley's ultimate goal was to have the school enlarged to hold 160 children. Ferrier to Secretary, DIA, June 11, 1915, RG10, vol. 6268, file 581-1, pt. 1, LAC.

14. Stewart, "Monthly Report of the Norway House Boarding School, Apr. 30, 1915"; "Extract from Report from Agent Jones on Norway House Boarding School, dated June 30, 1916"; and William Gordon, Indian Agent, to [A.F. MacKenzie], Assistant Deputy and Secretary, DIA, Oct. 7, 1925—all in RG10, vol. 6268, file 581-1, pt. 1, LAC.

15. Stewart, "Monthly Report of the Norway House Boarding School, Apr. 30, 1915"; Stewart to Duncan C. Scott, Deputy SGIA, June 15, 1915; John R. Bunn, Inspector of Indian Agencies, to Scott, Sept. 24, 1915; W.W. Shoup, principal, to MacKenzie, Jan. 5, 1932—all in RG10, vol. 6268, file 581-1, pt. 1, LAC.

16. MacKenzie to Gordon, Sept. 23, 1925, RG10, vol. 6268, file 581-1, pt. 1, LAC.

17. Lousley to Jacob Berens, Chief, Jan. 16, 1916; J.A. Lousley to T.H. Carter, Indian Agent, Aug. 11, 1915; and Carter to Scott, Mar. 11, 1916—all in RG10, vol. 6268, file 581-1, pt. 1, LAC.

18. Berens to Bunn, Jan. 12, 1916, and Lousley to Berens, Jan. 16, 1916, both in RG10, vol. 6268, file 581-1, pt. 1, LAC.

19. Berens to Lousley, Feb. 20, 1916; Carter to Scott, Mar. 11, 1916; Ferrier to Secretary, DIA, July 17, 1916—all in RG10, vol. 6268, file 581-1, pt. 1, LAC.

20. R.T. Chapin, principal, to P.G. Lazenby, Indian Agent, June 21, 1935, RG10, vol. 6269, file 581-10, LAC.

21. MacKenzie to P.G. Lazenby, Indian Agent, July 17, 1935, RG10, vol. 6269, file 581-10, LAC.

22. May, "A Northern Adventure."

23. "Extract from Annual Report, E.J. Hardiman to SGIA," RG10, vol. 6268, file 581-1, pt. 1, LAC.

24. Lousley to Frank Pedley, Deputy SGIA, Apr. 9, 1910, RG10, vol. 6268, file 581-1, pt. 1, LAC.

25. John Semmens, Inspector of Indian Agencies, to David Laird, Indian Commissioner, Sept. 7, 1907, RG10, vol. 6268, file 581-1, pt. 1. See also C.C. Caverley, Indian Agent, to Laird, Apr. 9, 1907; Chief [Sinclair] to Laird, Feb. 14, [1907]; [J.A.J. McKenna], Assistant Indian Commissioner to Semmens, July 3, 1907; Ferrier to McKenna, report, [c. July 30, 1907]; and Martin Benson, Schools Division, to Deputy SGIA, Sept. 28, 1907—all in RG10, vol. 6268, file 581-1, pt. 1, LAC.

26. Semmens to Laird, Sept. 7, 1907.

27. Ferrier to Secretary, DIA, July 24, 1915, RG10, vol. 6268, file 581–1, pt. 1, LAC.

28. Stewart, "Monthly Report of the Norway House Boarding School, Apr. 30, 1915."

29. Shoup to McKenzie, Jan. 13, 1934, RG10, vol. 6269, file 581-10, LAC.

30. A.H. Allard, C.C. RCMP, Manitoba District to Commissioner, RCMP, Ottawa, Report on Conclusion of Case, RG10, vol. 6288, file 581-1, pt. 1, LAC.

31. R.L. Steveston to R.B. Cochrane, Feb. 27, 1934, acc. 83.050c, box 18, file 185, United Church of Canada Archives (UCCA).

32. Ibid.; V.N. Trupel, Medical Superintendent, Norway House Hospital, to [Secretary and Executive of the Mission Board], Feb. 9, 1934, RG10, vol. 6268, file 581-1, pt. 2, LAC.

33. Melissa Stoops, "Health Conditions at Norway House Residential School, 1900–1946," M.A. thesis, McMaster University, Jan. 1, 2006, p. 91. Available online at http://digitalcommons.mcmaster.ca/cgi/viewcontent.cgi?article=6495&context=opendissertations.

34. E.L. Stone, *Health and Disease at the Norway House Indian Agency*, 1925, Hudson's Bay Company Archives, Provincial Archives of Manitoba, A.95/53, p. 256, cited in Stoops, 16.

35. Lousely to SGIA, Aug. 8, 1903, DIA annual reports, 1903, pp. 336–337.

36. Shoup to MacKenzie, Jan. 5, 1932.

37. Ibid.

38.   R.T. Chapin, "Memoirs of a Happy Journey Through Life," 1972, Ex-89, no. 3070, UCC Manitoba and N.W. Ontario Conference Archives, as cited in Stoops, 96.

39.   Stewart to Sir, June 19, 1915, RG10, vol. 6268, file 581-1, pt. 1, LAC.

40.   John R. Bunn, Inspector of Indian Agencies, to Duncan C. Scott, Deputy SGIA, Sept. 24, 1915, RG10, vol. 6268, file 581-1, pt. 1, LAC.

41.   George F. Denyes to Secretary, DIA, Aug. 28, 1919, RG10, vol. 6269, file 581-10, LAC. Regarding destruction of the graveyard and community responses, see Ferrier, "Report of the Work at Norway House," RG10, vol. 6268, file 581-1, pt. 1, LAC.

42.   Canada, P.C. 863, May 18, 1923, RG10, vol. 6269, file 581-10, LAC.

43.   R.L. Steveston to Rev. R.B. Cochrane, Feb. 27, 1934, access. 83.050c, box 18, file 185, UCCA.

44.   Cochrane to R.A. Hoey, Superintendent of Welfare and Training, Indian Affairs, Dec. 3, 1941, RG10, vol. 6268, file 581-1, pt. 1, LAC.

45.   Brian Ronden, supervisor and housemaster, Norway House IRS, diary, 1963–1964, 509/3, file 20, UCC Manitoba and N.W. Ontario Conference Archives.

46.   "Extract from letter of Wm. Gordon, Indian Agent, Norway House, Dated July 2, 1923," RG10, vol. 6268, file 581-1, pt. 1, LAC.

47.   Shoup to DIA, June 230, 1934, RG10, vol. 6269, file 581-10, LAC.

48.   Lazenby to Secretary, DIA, July 17, 1937, RG10, vol. 6269, file 581-10, LAC.

49.   Lazenby to Secretary, DIA, April 25, 1935, RG10, vol. 6269, file 581-10, LAC.

50.   J.W. Henley, Personnel Manager, Hudson's Bay Company, to Caldwell, RG10, vol. 6268, file 581-1, pt. 2, LAC.

51.   Chapin to Philip Phelan, Chief Training Division, DIA, July 6, 1940, RG10, vol. 6269, file 581-10, LAC.

52.   Hoey to Acting Deputy Minister, May 29, 1946, RG10, vol. 6268, file 581-1, pt. 2, LAC.

53.   Byron Apetagon, *Norway House Anthology: Stories of the Elders* (Winnipeg: Frontier School Division No. 48, 1991), vol. 1, p. 51.

54.   J. Freeman, Chair, Special Committee, Hudson Bay Presbytery, "Report Re: Future Policy of the United Church in Relation to Day Schools, Residential Schools and Their Administration in Indian Communities," November 1965, 503-9, file 1, UCC Manitoba and N.W. Ontario Conference Archives.

55.   Hoey to Director, Lands and Services, Nov. 20, 1947, RG10, vol. 6268, file 581-1, pt. 2, LAC.

56.   Freeman, "Report Re: Future Policy."

57.   May, "A Northern Adventure."

58.   E.E.M. Joblin to R.F. Davey, Education Services, Indian Affairs Branch, Dec. 20, 1965, file 123/25-1-5, DIAND Residential Schools Records Office.

Acknowledgements

As Richard Wagamese says in his novel *Indian Horse,* "It takes time to write a book, and none of us ever really do it alone."

The first person I must acknowledge is Edward Gamblin, who had started his own book. When he died, I decided to help him finish it, since I had many letters, emails, diary entries and cards to go on. I have done the best I could with this book. Thank you, Edward, for your friendship, knowledge and wisdom.

To my niece Barbara Grexton goes the next credit, because she phoned from Grandview, Manitoba, saying, "Every Manitoban should go to Churchill," and invited me to go along. Her comment, "And we could take a trip to Norway House where you taught in 1954," was the kernel of the book to come.

Thank you to the Honourable Justice Murray Sinclair for his presentation to the Senate Committee on Aboriginal Peoples on September 28, 2010, in which he said, "Edward Gamblin and Florence Kaefer walked the long road from apology to forgiveness to reconciliation. They recognized that apology is not an end in itself. Reconciliation takes time."

Thank you to Rick Roschuk for giving me Edward's phone number that first day and for supplying me with many of Edward's CDs, as well as for permission to quote from these songs from your recording company.

To Duncan McCue, CBC reporter, thank you for your concern for Edward's health and your emails of support. And thanks to the CBC for granting us permission to print the transcript of the interview with Duncan.

I also wish to acknowledge Cecile Fausak, liaison minister for residential schools for the United Church. We spent many hours talking on the phone about the schools, which helped me to formulate what I needed to do for reconciliation.

Special thanks to Mary Starodub and her husband, Karl, of Winnipeg, who met me at the airport, took me home and welcomed me as long as I needed to stay. They took me to visit Edward in the hospital and drove me back and forth to the airport, whether I was flying to Norway House or going home. I never could have done it without their generous, endless hospitality.

A warm thank-you to Stephie Tarnowsky, who taught with me in Norway House, for her financial support and constant cheerleading, now from Nova Scotia.

I would also like to thank Keith Johnson for giving me permission to use his wonderful photographs from the 1950s.

Thank you to my sister Lorna Barclay for going to Norway House with me and supporting me as I went to Edward's funeral and helping me with his eulogy. Thanks also for the time she and her family visited Edward in the hospital after his leg amputation and for providing a welcoming stay for me at her home on trips to and from Norway House.

A special thank-you to my many editors, beginning with Kendra Brown, an excellent English teacher and writer herself from Courtenay who was the first to correct my attempts and guide me. And then the Scribbling Scribes, a writing group of friends who meet in each other's houses. They had their pencils ready to jot down the problems I had with clarity as I presented my weekly writing. You know who you are. To all of you, thank you.

Writing this book took a great deal of time, effort and emotional input. I was helped immensely by the adeptness of my final editor, Barbara Pulling of Vancouver.

And thank you, too, to my typists, since I am definitely of the old school of handwriting, cut and paste, and white-out.

Thank you very much to my hiking friend Kate Piece, an expert on computers, who typed up my beginning work so capably. Thank you Sally Allan, who also typed my efforts so professionally, making many trips back and forth to my house, rain or shine, for the latest chapter. Thank you to Phil Umperville, who translated the Cree verse of "Survivor's Voice." And to my professional typist, Joy Woodsworth, who prepared the final manuscript, thank you.

Thank you to my son Glenn for getting my computer happily running again after I'd done "something" to it while doing research or printing.

Thank you, grandson Owen, for your support.

And finally, thank you to my publisher Vici Johnstone and the team at Caitlin Press.

Since reconnecting with Edward Gamblin, I have gone on a spiritual journey. He taught me how to pray to the Creator, and this I often did by going down to the foot of my garden, leaning against my huge Garry oak tree and asking the Creator for guidance and help.

Thanking a tree, especially one that is over a hundred years old, and has stood firmly through wind, storm, rain and gentle summer breeze, and at night with Mother Moon shining through her outstretched arms, I know is pleasing to the Creator. When I see the moon shining on my old oak tree, I think of a song I learned in an educational summer school class many years ago:

I see the moon
The moon sees me
Down through the leaves
Of the old oak tree
Please let the light that shines on me
Shine on the ones I love.

Edward Gamblin, Cree, was born in Cross Lake, Manitoba, on May 17, 1948, to Wilfred Roscoe Gamblin and Jane Mary Gamblin (née Sinclair). He soon ended up in a foster placement in Cross Lake with a kind older couple, Mr. and Mrs. Sandy Monias. They were Christian people.

At age five, in 1954, Edward was sent to the United Church Residential School in Norway House, and then to the United Church Residential School in Portage la Prairie, where he continued until grade 10. He was physically, sexually, culturally and psychologically abused in both schools for eleven years. Later he went back to school, finishing grade 12 and then going on to the University of Manitoba. He became an addictions counsellor and a band counsellor, but most of all he was a musician. He sang for his people.

Edward married Aurelia Monias (above with Edward) in 1970 and they had six children. He died on July 27, 2010, just months after his beloved Aurelia.

Florence Kaefer (née Pockett), was born in Spirit River, Alberta, in 1935. She, her mother and her two sisters moved to Winnipeg, Manitoba, when Florence was in grade 6. During her teenage years, she attended an active Young People's Group at Young United Church.

Florence graduated from Normal School in Tuxedo, a suburb of Winnipeg, in June 1954. For her first three years of teaching, she taught at the United Church Indian Residential School in Norway House, Manitoba, and then for another three years at the United Church Residential School in Alberni, BC, where she met and married Gerd Kaefer, also a teacher. They had two sons, Ian and Glenn. Florence completed thirty years of teaching in Courtenay, BC, where she still lives, in 1990.

Erratum: The photograph at the top left of the page is a picture of Edward Gamblin and his cousin, Isabel Ross, not Aurelia as identified in the text.